EXPLOSIVE FOOTBALL
WITH THE
MULTI-BONE ATTACK

Tony DeMeo

Parker Publishing Company, Inc.

West Nyack, New York

Library of Congress Cataloging in Publication Data

DeMeo, Tony
    Explosive football with the multi-bone attack.

    Includes index.
    1. Football—Offense.   2.   Football coaching.
I.   Title.
GV951.8.D45   796.332′2   80-16221
ISBN 0-13-297952-7

How This Book Will Help You

Explosive Football with the Multi-Bone Attack is a complete guide to the most powerful and diversified offense in football today. The Multi-Bone combines the explosiveness of the Veer, the power of the I, the deception and misdirection of the Wing T, the ball control consistency of the Wishbone, and the wide open play of the Pro Dropback Passing Attack.

This book takes you step by step through every detail of this intriguing style of offensive play. It explains how to tie completely polarized styles of offensive football into one unique, explosive, high scoring attack. The Multi-Bone attack adjusts itself to take advantage of your personnel without changing the structure of the offense. The result is an offense that can change from a conservative ball-control attack to a wide open attack and vice versa in the middle of a game.

You will discover all the secrets and coaching points of an attack which:

1) averaged six yards per rushing attempt;
2) averaged 30 points per game;
3) averaged 387 yards per game;
4) averaged 21 first downs per game;
5) broke 30 school records.

Included are the actual quarterback, backfield, receiver and line techniques described in simple learning progressions that allow the maximum use of practice time.

Explosive Football with the Multi-Bone Attack takes the problem out of option football with an option style that is very simple. It teaches your quarterback how to attack every type of defensive end.

A supplementary power attack that can totally devastate "reading defenses" is one of the weapons offered in the Multi-Bone package.

This unique offense also includes a simple misdirection Wing T-style series that allows you to capitalize on defensive adjustments to stop the triple option.

The Multi-Bone offense has a triple-action passing attack which helps you score quickly and/or maintain possession of the football in third down "must" situations. This book explains the use of high-percentage low risk patterns, how to avoid blitzes, and how to take advantage of secondary coverages. It also shows how to coordinate the Multi-Bone passing attack with the Multi-Bone running game.

Also included in *Explosive Football with the Multi-Bone Attack* is a complete playbook attacking the six most popular defenses in football.

The complete theory of attacking defenses with the Multi-Bone is explained in depth. You are taught how to use the Multi-Concept to take advantage of a defense's weakness. Actual game plans even are prepared for you.

Though the amount of talent is a major factor in the success of a team, the Multi-Bone will allow you to make the most of your talent. This book will enable you to adjust the Multi-Bone to fit your players.

Explosive Football with the Multi-Bone Attack will show you how to successfully tie together the best of several offenses into one easy-to-learn package. The uniting of these diversified styles of attack will provide defenses with too many problems to possibly defend against.

Tony DeMeo

CONTENTS

CHAPTER 1

Creating the Multi-Bone Attack

The Multi-Bone Attack is an offense that evolved from a number of ideas and objectives that our coaching staff wanted to reach. The offense would have the following characteristics:

1) It would feature the triple option—the single best play in football.
2) It could easily adapt to existing talent.
3) It would include misdirection which, coupled with the triple option, would produce an entire running package.
4) The dropback pass would fit into the scheme.
5) A few well-run plays, with simple adjustments, would allow enough time to perfect execution.
6) The offense could always exploit a defensive adjustment made to stop the basic plays.
7) The offense would always have multiple ways to running the same series to prevent a more talented team from stopping it.

Taking these objectives into consideration, the staff explored the popular offensive packages: the Delaware Wing T, the Splitback Veer, the I Formation, the Dropback Pro style attack, and the Wishbone. Each attack had a feature that was a major selling point. The Wing T featured misdirection and deception. The explosiveness of the dive play in the Splitback Veer attack is very attractive. The power generated by the I Formation has certainly been productive over the years. Watching a Pro game on a Sunday can sell anyone on a Pro Style of attack, and the power of the Wishbone has made Texas, Oklahoma, and Alabama big winners.

The talent available led to the final choice. The following facts led us to choose the Wishbone:

1) We did not have a returning quarterback. A safety was converted to quarterback. Thus the Pro Style attack was eliminated.

2) We did not have any proven tailbacks. The two starting halfbacks had never played halfback before.

3) We did have a good fullback, one that the offense should feature.

4) We had a line with some size but without the quick guards needed to run the Wing T attack.

5) The offense had to feature the triple option which also is not conducive to the Wing T.

6) The offense desired was one that was adaptable and could be built on without having to change completely from year to year.

7) We had an excellent defensive unit that would keep the score close and give the offense the ball in four down territory, thus the need for a great goal line attack. (The Wishbone is considered the best goal line attack in football).

Hence, the decision to install the Wishbone attack which evolved into the Multi-Bone

THE EVOLUTION OF THE MULTI-BONE

There were strengths or pieces from other offenses that made those particular attacks very successful. The idea was to incorporate these strengths with the basic Wishbone to form an offense that was:

1) built around the Wishbone;
2) completely versatile and flexible;
3) the greatest problem for a defense to prepare for in one week;
4) simple to teach.

The first step, and the easiest, was to have more than one set. This involved no teaching because it merely took the simple substitution of a second split end for a halfback to create a broken bone set, a split end for a tight end to create a wide set, or a tight end for a split end to create a tight set. The formations that best fit into the attack were:

1) the basic set (Diagram 1-1);
2) the tight set (Diagram 1-2);
3) the wide set (Diagram 1-3);
4) the Twin Bone (Diagram 1-4) which was borrowed from Lou Holtz;
5) the Pro Bone (Diagram 1-5) which was borrowed from the Pros;
6) the heavy sets which placed the halfback and flanker to the same side (Diagrams 1-6 and 1-7).

DIAGRAMS FOR THE MULTI BONE CONCEPT

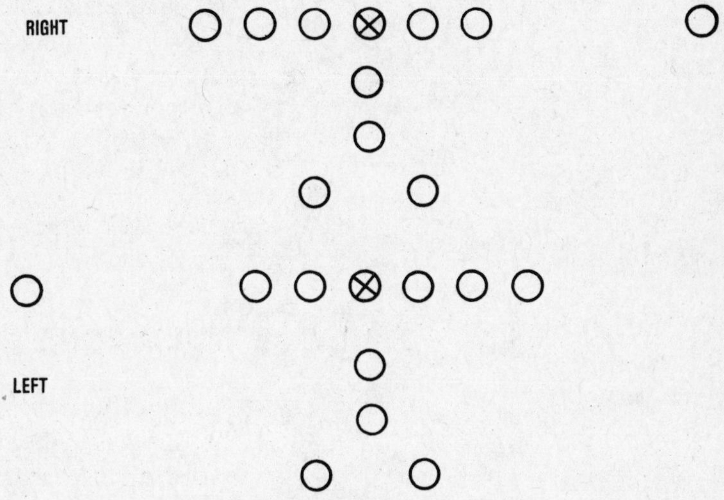

Diagram 1-1

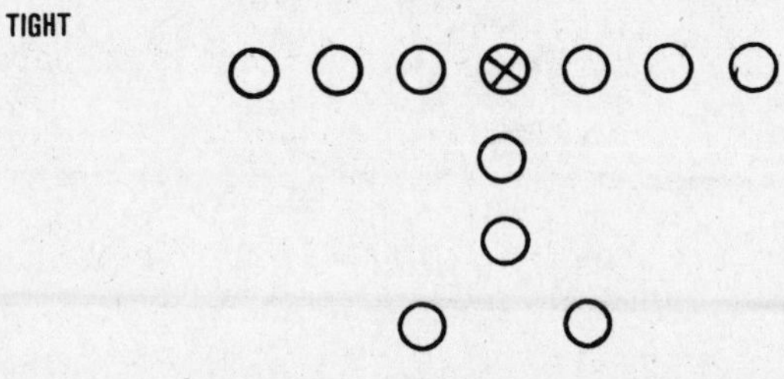

Diagram 1-2

CREATING THE MULTI-BONE ATTACK

DIAGRAMS FOR THE MULTI BONE CONCEPT

WIDE

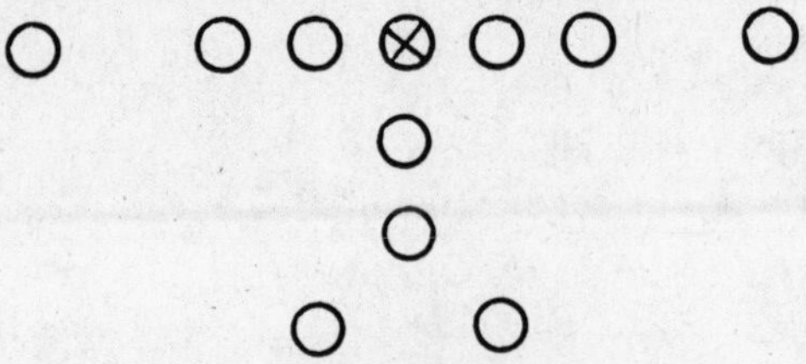

Diagram 1-3

TWIN BONE

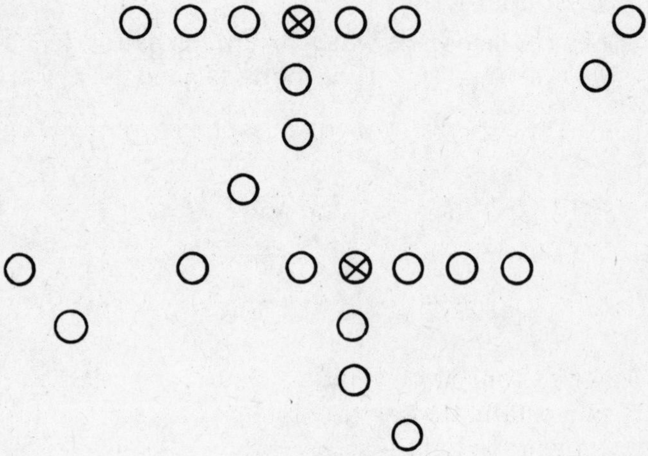

Diagram 1-4

PRO BONE

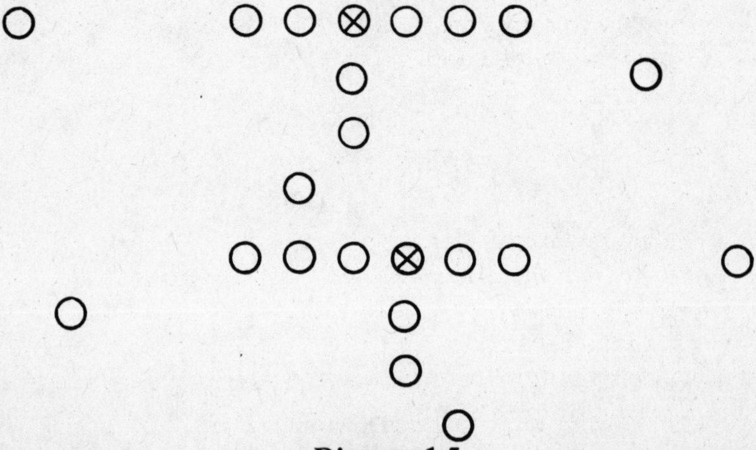

Diagram 1-5

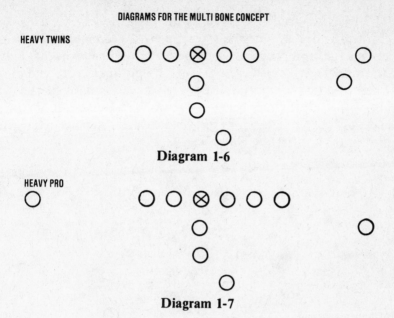

DIAGRAMS FOR THE MULTI BONE CONCEPT

HEAVY TWINS

Diagram 1-6

HEAVY PRO

Diagram 1-7

THE MULTI-WISHBONE

The Multi-Bone has two variations of the basic full Wishbone with one split end. In the first variation a tight end is substituted for the split end and the tight set is used. The set emphasizes the power attack or, in a short yardage situation, it puts an extra big, strong blocker in the game.

The second variation is the substitution of a second split end for the tight end when the wide set is used. This set makes it difficult for the secondary to rotate against the offense or to play a hard corner. It also puts two wide receivers in the game without breaking the bone.

THE BROKEN BONE

There are several reasons for breaking the bone. The main reason is to put three receivers on the line of scrimmage, which enhances the passing game. Breaking the bone also helps the running game because it creates different blocking match-ups, creates a recognition problem, and spreads the defense. It also requires no additional learning because a second split end is simply substituted for a running back.

The first broken bone set is the Twin Bone. This set provides two wide outs to the same side, puts three receivers on the line of scrimmage, and provides a number of combo patterns that help the passing attack. It also spreads out an eight-man front and dictates where the strong safety must go in a seven-man front. The triple option can be run to either side (Diagrams 1-8 and 1-9). To the tight end side, the halfback takes the same "whirley step" as in the whirley bird option of the veer offense.

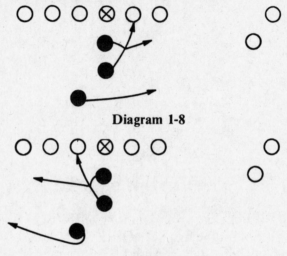

Diagram 1-8

Diagram 1-9

A variation of the Twin Bone is the Flex Twins (Diagram 1-10). This set provides a third wide receiver, forces a team to go to a four deep, and makes rotation very difficult. It also allows the offense to run the triple option to either side.

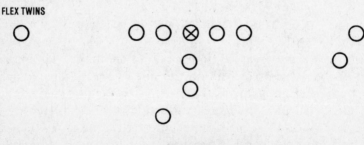

Diagram 1-10

The other broken bone set is the Pro Bone. The Pro Bone also puts three receivers on the line of scrimmage and provides two wide receivers to enhance the passing game. It allows for the sprint out to either side of the formation with a wide receiver to that side. The Pro Bone places the tight end in position to block the strong safety (Diagram 1-11). It is also effective when the lead blocker is having trouble blocking the strong safety.

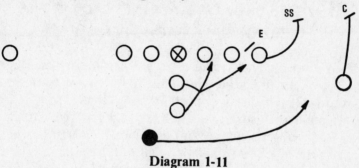

Diagram 1-11

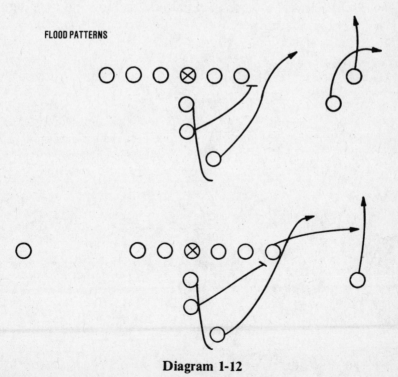

Diagram 1-12

The "heavy call" is a variation used in all broken bone sets. This provides an extra receiver in a flood-type pattern (Diagram 1-12) while the triple option can still be run to either side.

None of the broken bone sets make it necessary for any additional teaching as far as technique or skills are concerned. A player must learn only the names of the sets.

WHY THE BROKEN BONE INSTEAD OF THE I OR SPLITBACK VEER?

By keeping the backs in a broken bone instead of keeping them in an I, the offense maintains the ability to run the quick-hitting dive (Diagram 1-13). This is an important ingredient in the Multi-Bone and was popularized by Lou Holtz's Splitback Veer attack. The adaptation was very simple and provided the Multi-Bone with straight-ahead quickness similar to that of the Splitback Veer. The quick-hitting dive also provides another way of moving the football in keeping with the basic philosophy of multiplicity. The halfback can still be released on a passing pattern, and it is not necessary to teach a two-point stance.

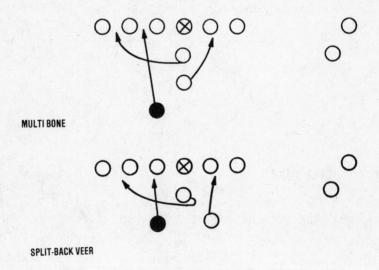

MULTI BONE

SPLIT-BACK VEER

Diagram 1-13

The next step was to develop a simple dropback passing attack that could easily be incorporated with the triple option. Homer

Rice's passing package was the answer. A simple adaptation from Coach Rice's splitback attack to the Multi-Bone was the only change made to provide a possession passing package similar to a Pro style attack (Diagram 1-14).

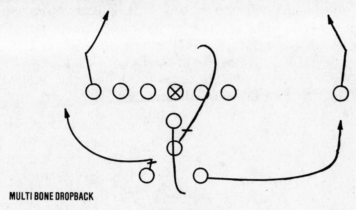

MULTI BONE DROPBACK

Diagram 1-14

Every time U.S.C. appeared on TV, the need for a power sweep attack seemed more evident. The result was to incorporate the inside belly popularized by Bobby Dodd at Georgia Tech and a power sweep borrowed directly from John McKay's I attack (Diagram 1-15).

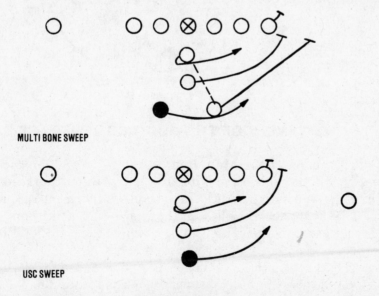

MULTI BONE SWEEP

USC SWEEP

Diagram 1-15

The final ingredient was a counter attack which is of extreme importance to an option-oriented attack to slow down pursuit.

In addition to basic Wishbone counters, the use of the word "opposite" provided an instant counter attack for the entire offense. "Opposite" simply tells the fullback that he goes in the opposite direction of the play and the quarterback reverse pivots. For example, "Belly Opposite" would appear as Diagram 1-16. This bears a very close resemblance to the Delaware buck sweep.

Thus the basic Wishbone evolved into the Multi-Bone combining the best of the Wishbone, Splitback Veer, Pro Style passing game, the I Formation and the Delaware Wing T with a few very simple adjustments.

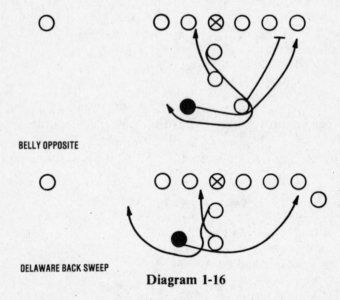

BELLY OPPOSITE

DELAWARE BACK SWEEP

Diagram 1-16

OVERVIEW OF THE MULTI-BONE ATTACK

The basis of the Multi-Bone is the triple option. The triple option will be run with multiple blocking schemes and reads until the defense makes a radical or unsound adjustment that can be exploited with another phase of the attack. The Multi-Bone forces the defense to commit itself to stopping the triple option from a variety of sets, blocking schemes and reads.

The supplementary Multi-Bone running game is devoted to exploiting any possible adjustment the defense might make to stop the triple option. The supplementary running game also must provide an alternative to the triple option.

The other key to the success of the Multi-Bone is the total commitment to a multiple passing game. The importance of the passing game to the Multi-Bone can be shown by the fact that we devote 40 percent of practice time to throwing the football. The combination of a play action passing game, a dropback passing game and a sprint passing game provides a multiple passing attack. To be successful, it is paramount to convert long yardage situations and that means the development of a possession passing attack. Play action passes are not the answer when it's third and ten. To summarize:

The key ingredients of the Multi-Bone concept are:

1) The triple option is run with multiple blocking schemes, reads and sets.

2) The power attack provides a good short yardage attack with minimal practice.

3) The counter attack provides a sound alternative to the triple option with very little teaching.

4) The supplementary running game provides multiple styles of ground attacks that are very simple. This leaves a lot of practice time to devote to the triple option and the passing game.

5) The passing game is part of the game plan, not a desperation move.

6) The passing game has the same multiplicity as the running game by having a play action passing attack, a dropback attack, and a sprint pass.

7) The passing game remains simple by making the routes universal to all actions.

8) By using a multiple passing game along with a multiple running attack, the Multi-Bone becomes explosive and extremely difficult to defend.

THE INITIAL MECHANICS OF THE MULTI-BONE

The Huddle

The huddle that easily fits into the Multi-Bone attack is a simple choir-boy huddle, but any huddle could easily be used.

Calling the Play

The plays are called in this manner: formation, name of the play, direction, and any blocking variation. For example, Right-Belly, Left, Zone on One. That play would look like Diagram 1-17.

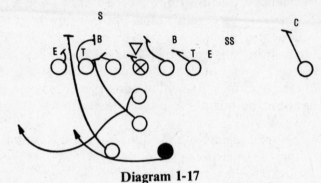

Diagram 1-17

Snap Count

Any snap count will do the job. A simple down, set, hut-hut . . . is fine.

Alignment

The success of any phase of football begins with alignment and position. Although several different formations are used, some parts of these formations remain constant.

Line Splits

Line splits usually are not varied because the offensive linemen are used as aiming points for the offensive backs. The quarterback's timing and the complete timing of the play can be thrown off if the line splits are not kept constant.

The guards take a two-foot split from center with their helmets even with the center's shoulders. The tackles split three feet from the guard, and their hands are even with the hands of the guard next to them (Diagram 1-18).

Receivers' Splits

The splits of the receivers vary quite a bit from play to play. The tight end starts out with a three-foot split from the tackle, but in

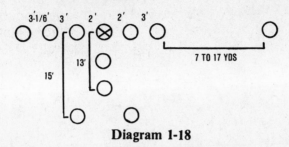

Diagram 1-18

some situations he might move to as much as a six-foot split to spread out a front.

The split end varies from a seven-yard split to a 17-yard split. Against a two- or three-deep secondary he takes the maximum split. If the split end is to the short side of the field with the ball on the hash mark, he splits the difference between the sideline and the offensive tackle. If the ball is on the hash mark and the end splits to the wide side of the field, the split end lines up on the other hash mark.

If a flanker is used, he follows the same basic rules as the split end except when he is split to the short side of the field. Then he splits the difference between the side line and the tight end.

When a slot is used he usually lines up six yards from the split end and one yard back behind the line of scrimmage. If the twin set is used to the short side of the field with the ball on the hash mark, the slot tries to split the difference between the tackle and the split end.

Backfield Alignment

The halfback and fullback alignments are always the same no matter what set is used. The fullback lines up directly behind the quarterback with his feet 13 feet from the ball. The halfbacks align directly behind the guards with their feet two feet deeper than the fullback's feet. All the backs are in a three-point stance.

CHAPTER 2

The Multi-Triple Options

INTRODUCTION TO THE TRIPLE OPTION

Every offense must have one play that is the heart and soul of the entire attack. Green Bay had its power sweep, and we have the Multi-Triple Option. Every opponent must be totally committed to stopping this play. It is the play that we hang our hat on.

We chose the Multi-Triple Option because it is an entire attack in itself. The triple option attacks inside with the give to the fullback, off tackle with the quarterback keep, and outside with the pitch to the halfback. This play is to football what the fast break is to basketball.

The triple option forces the secondary to be so involved with the running game that it cannot do a satisfactory job on the pass. The triple option allows an offense to beat teams without overpowering them. This is its greatest advantage. The offensive line does not have to block the defensive tackles or ends. It is possible to double team a troublesome middle guard. So with small, quick offensive linemen a team can get enough position to control the pursuit and create a numbers advantage in the perimeter. The triple option is the great equalizer in football because it allows you to run the football and play ball control without having a big offensive line.

LINE BLOCKING FOR THE TRIPLE OPTION

In keeping with the philosophy of multiplicity in every area of the offense, there are three basic ways of blocking the interior for the

26

triple options. The purpose of these blocking schemes is to isolate the hand-off key and create a crease for the fullback.

Veer Blocking

The basic blocking scheme is veer blocking. The approach to each game is to use veer blocking the majority of the time because it handles all stunts and fronts (Diagrams 2-1 and 2-2). Unless there is an advantage to using another scheme, veer blocking is used.

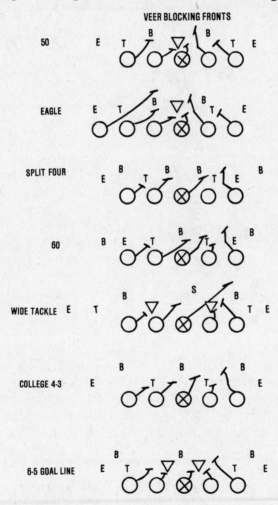

Diagram 2-1

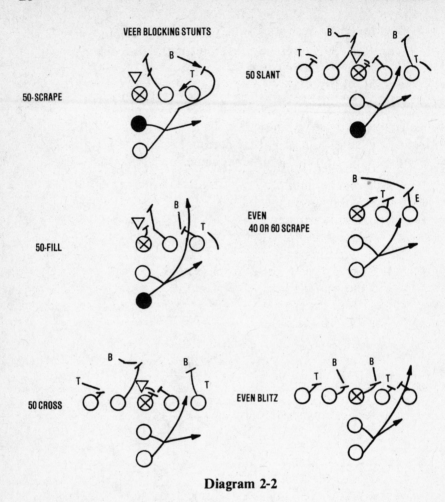

Diagram 2-2

Veer Blocking Rules

Veer blocking is taught by the "Path Theory", as are all the blocking schemes. The Path Theory is simply this: Stay on your path and never let anyone cross your face. For veer blocking the onside line (guard and tackle) takes a down path.

ONSIDE GUARD RULES AND TECHNIQUES

The rule for the onside guard is to block the first man on the line of scrimmage to the play side of the center. The techniques he uses vary, depending on whether it is an odd or even front.

Against an odd front there are five situations an onside guard will encounter: 1) a nose guard stunting toward him; 2) a nose guard stunting away from him; 3) a nose guard sitting and reading on whom the center does not have good position; 4) a nose guard sitting and reading on whom the center does have good position; and 5) a nose guard and linebacker stacked on the center's head. If the nose guard jumps in the gap, it is treated as an even front.

The onside guard's aiming point is the near hip of the nose guard. If that hip moves away from him, the guard goes directly for the backside backer. If the hip comes toward him, he forgets about the backside backer and blocks the nose guard. If the noseguard is sitting and reading and the guard can see his numbers, he fires into him with his inside arm and throws his forearm into the nose guard. He then fires straight upfield to pick up the backside backer. If the nose guard is sitting and reading and the guard cannot see his numbers, he goes directly for the backside backer. Finally, if there is a stack on the center's head, the guard's first step is to the nose guard's near hip. Unless he sees the hip come toward him, he fires directly upfield for the stacked linebacker (Diagram 2-3).

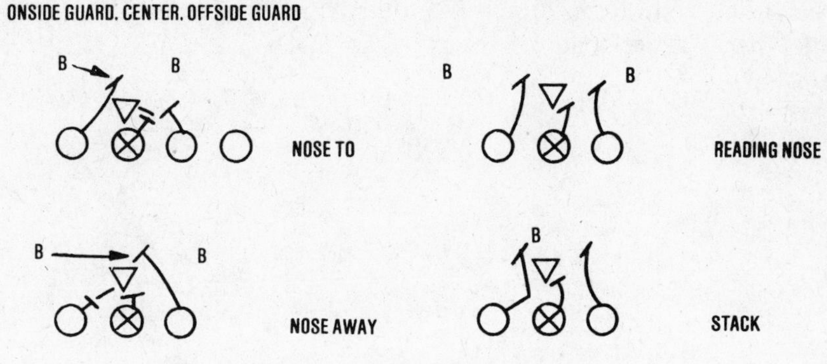

ONSIDE GUARD. CENTER. OFFSIDE GUARD

NOSE TO

READING NOSE

NOSE AWAY

STACK

Diagram 2-3

Against an even front, the onside guard aims for the playside hip of the first down lineman to the playside of the center. He may be in a head-on position as in a 6-1 or on the guard's outside shoulder as in a Notre Dame Split Four look. Or he may be in his inside gap as in a goal line defense (Diagram 2-1). His technique is to get outside position on the down man and maintain it. If the man is on his outside shoulder, he will get help from the offensive tackle similar to the help the center gets from the guard on the nose guard.

ONSIDE TACKLE'S RULES AND TECHNIQUES

The onside tackle's basic rule is to come down on the first man to his inside on or off the line of scrimmage.

Against an odd front, the onside tackle may block a reading linebacker, a filling linebacker, a tackle pinching across his face, or a tackle playing inside on an Eagle technique (Diagram 2-4). The onside tackle's technique is simple; He takes a lead step with his inside foot and fires through the inside knee of the man playing over him. He also rips his outside arm through and whips his backside leg past the defender and upfield. If the defensive tackle is playing a normal 50 technique, he will try to prevent the tackle from getting to the backer so he must fight upfield to the backer. If he does not get resistance from the defensive tackle on his course down on the backer, he should be alert for a filling backer and should react by driving his far shoulder through the backer's near hip to prevent penetration. If the defensive tackle is pinching and crosses the tackle's face, he merely drives him down the line of scrimmage. His normal path will force him to do this. Against an eagle technique, the tackle just blocks him as he would a pinching tackle (Diagram 2-4). This is a pre-snap pinch (Diagram 2-4).

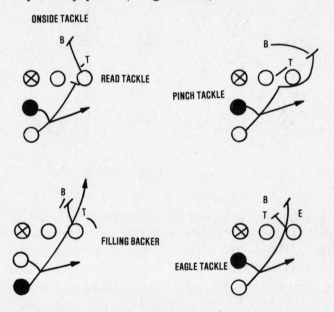

Diagram 2-4

Against even fronts the onside tackle uses the same combo block that the guard and center use on the nose guard. The tackle comes down on the man on the guard, and if he sees his numbers, he slams his inside forearm into him and then goes upfield for the backer. If he does not see his numbers, he goes directly for the backer (Diagram 2-5).

Diagram 2-5

THE CENTER'S RULES AND TECHNIQUES

The center has the man on or the playside linebacker. He double teams the nose guard if the nose guard slants to the play with the onside guard. He double teams the nose guard with the offside guard if the nose guard slants away from the play. If the nose guard sits and reads, the center will get help from the onside guard but will fight to get playside position on the nose guard (Diagram 2-3).

Against an even front, the center is responsible for blocking the front side linebacker in a Split 4 and the middle backer in a 6.1 or 4.3 setup. Against a Wide Tackle Six, he goes for the safety (Diagram 2-1).

> **Coaching Point:** Against a Split 4, the center may never get the onside backer, but by aiming for him he will be assured of getting the backside backer.

OFFSIDE LINE RULES AND TECHNIQUES

The offside guard fires out at a 30 degree angle and sprints down field without letting anyone cross his path. Against an odd front, he reads the nose man; If the nose man comes toward the guard, he blocks him (Diagram 2-3). If the nose guard does anything else, he continues on his path and never lets anyone cross it. Most likely he will block the backside backer.

Against an even front, the offside guard fires out at a 30 degree angle and aims for the first linebacker to his side of the center. For example, in a 4.4 he would aim for the backside backer and in a 6.1

setup he would aim for the middle backer (Diagram 2-1). However, if the defensive tackle pinches, the offside guard would block him. In a 6.1, if the middle backer is gone, he continues on his path for the safety (Diagram 2-6). The only reason to block backside defensive linemen is if they slant to the play. The backside linemen will be able to block slanting linemen by staying on their path. A backside defensive lineman will not be a factor unless he is slanting to the play. If there is someone in his playside gap, the backside guard flattens his angle and drives into him preventing penetration (Diagram 2-6).

OFFSIDE GUARD

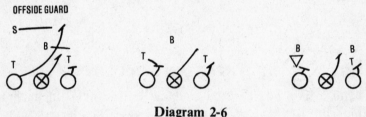

Diagram 2-6

The offside tackle takes off on a 45 degree angle downfield and blocks the first man to cross his path. He may block a pinching defensive tackle on his head, or a linebacker who is late in reacting, or a defensive back down field. The only exception is against a Split Four or any defense with a man on the outside shoulder of the guard or in the tackle-guard gap. Then the backside tackle takes off at a flat 25 degree angle and drives his shoulder into his playside hip on the line of scrimmage. He treats this lineman as though he were slanted (Diagram 2-7).

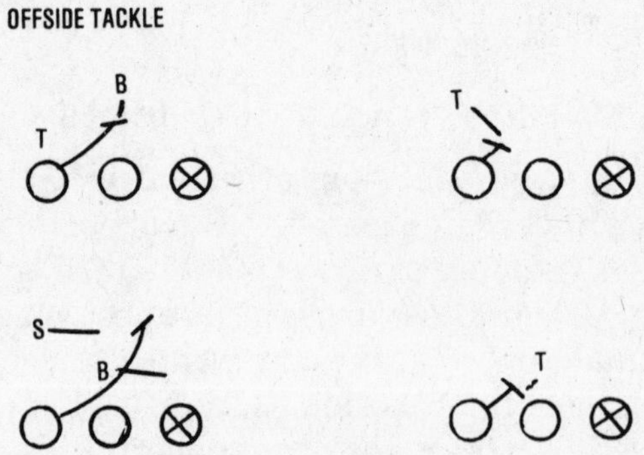

OFFSIDE TACKLE

Diagram 2-7

If there is a backside tight end, he follows the same rules and procedures as the backside tackle.

Zone Blocking

Zone blocking is the first change-up blocking scheme that is used to run the multi-triple options. Zone blocking is used if a linebacker is escaping into the perimeter. Although used primarily against a Fifty defense, it can also be used against a Split Four look and an Eagle look (Diagram 2-8).

Diagram 2-8

ONSIDE GUARD RULES AND TECHNIQUES

The onside guard steps to the first down defensive lineman from his head to the onside tackle's outside shoulder. He steps with his outside foot and reads the down lineman that he is stepping to. If the defensive lineman comes to him on a pinch move, he will know immediately and must block him or at least make a collision. If the down lineman does anything but come directly at the guard, he fires upfield for the onside backer (Diagram 2-9). If the down lineman is

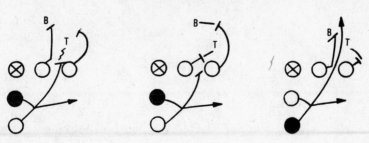

Diagram 2-9

lined up on the outside shoulder of the guard, he blocks him as he would in veer blocking except he gets help from the fullback instead of the onside tackle (Diagram 2-8).

ONSIDE TACKLE'S RULES AND TECHNIQUES

The onside tackle steps to the outside hip of the first down lineman from the guard's head to his outside shoulder. He tries to get directly on the playside backer. If the down man reacts with the tackle and steps outside with him, the tackle blocks him and the quarterback hands the ball to the fullback. If the down man pinches down, the tackle simply goes around him and picks up the scraping backer. If the down man sits and reads, the tackle gets his inside shoulder, forearm and leg past the defensive tackle's outside hip and gets upfield for the backer (Diagram 2-9). The guard will also go upfield for the backer so the quarterback will read the down man. Against a Split four look or an eagle look, when the down man is on the guard's outside shoulder, the tackle goes directly for the backer (Diagram 2-8).

BACKSIDE LINE RULES AND TECHNIQUES

Backside line technique is exactly the same as it is for veer blocking except for the center. Center technique in zone blocking is to fire out at the nose guard's outside hip at a 60° angle. If the nose guard slants away from the play, the center goes directly upfield and will probably block the backside backer (Diagram 2-10). The backside guard will block the nose guard. If the nose guard does anything else, the center blocks him. Against an even front the center uses the same technique as he does in veer blocking.

Diagram 2-10

"X" Blocking

"X" blocking is the second change-up blocking scheme. "X" blocking simply means that the tackle blocks down on the first man to his inside and the guard steps around his block and picks up the first man he finds except for the end man on the line of scrimmage. "X" blocking is used against a Split Four look as a change-up to the combo block, against a 50 eagle look, and sometimes against a normal 50 (Diagram 2-11).

"X" BLOCKING

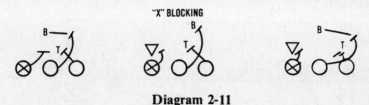

Diagram 2-11

GUARD'S TECHNIQUE

The guard takes a lead step with his outside foot and fires upfield, actually brushing the tackle's hip as the tackle crosses in front of him. Against an eagle and Split Four look, he avoids the end man on the line of scrimmage and looks inside for the inside backer. These are the types of defenses this is used against. Three things could happen against a normal 50 defense. The defensive tackle could be 1) pinching, 2) firing upfield, 3) sitting and reading (Diagram 2-12).

X BLOCKING ON 50

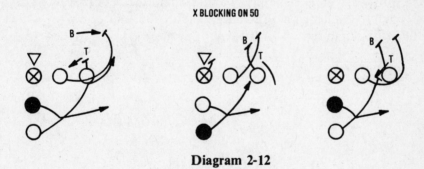

Diagram 2-12

This scheme is good if a team is pinching their tackle down to take the fullback away. In this situation the guard steps around the tackle's down block on the pinching tackle and blocks the scraping backer. If the defensive tackle fires upfield, the guard turns upfield and blocks the first person he sees. If the defensive tackle is sitting and reading, the guard will fire into him because if the defensive tackle closes down he will be in the guard's path. If he does not close down, it will be the same situation as if he had fired upfield.

The onside tackle follows his normal veer blocking rules except against a Split Four look. There is no combo block with the guard, naturally.

The offside line blocks according to the same rules as in zone blocking.

End Blocking for the Multi-Triple Option

The ends play an important role in the success of the triple options. The block of an end can make the difference between a good play and a great plan.

There are four different blocks for the ends: the stalk block, the crack block, the TED block and the hook block.

THE STALK BLOCK

The stalk block is the most important block for ends to learn. The first step in teaching the stalk block is to show the ends the different coverages he will face. He must know the difference between a three-deep and a four-deep secondary. Also, he must be able to recognize the difference between a rotating secondary and an inverting secondary. If the outside defender comes toward the line of scrimmage, it is called rotation. If the outside defender drops back, it is called a zone or man (Diagram 2-13). The ends know they must block the man who is in the deep third.

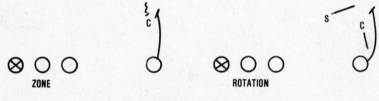

ZONE   ROTATION

Diagram 2-13

The actual stalk block technique is taught next. The first step of the stalk block is to explode off the line of scrimmage at top speed with head erect, recognizing the secondary. The end must push to get as much depth as possible. As he pushes deeper, he must widen and try to keep the defensive back inside and in front of him. As soon as the defender reacts to the play, the end breaks down and attacks the defender's outside breast. Once contact is made, the receiver must maintain control and never leave his feet. As long as the receiver is on his feet battling with the defender, our ball carrier can use the blocker to make a cutoff.

There are two key coaching points in the teaching of stalk blocking. First, if facing a three-deep secondary which tries to rotate, the split end must block the rotating corner (Diagram 2-14). Next, if a team tries to inhibit a tight end's release from the line of scrimmage, he should take a crossover step with his inside leg and rip his inside arm across the defender's face. He then takes three steps along the line of scrimmage before releasing downfield to stalk block (Diagram 2-15).

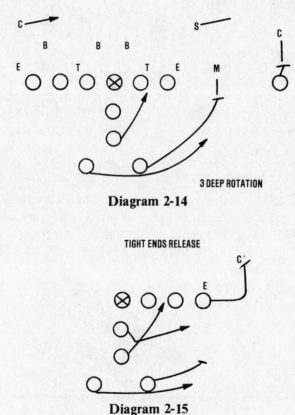

3 DEEP ROTATION

Diagram 2-14

TIGHT ENDS RELEASE

Diagram 2-15

THE CRACK BLOCK

The crack block is a down block by the split end on the defensive back who has the pitch. This block is used against secondaries that use an invert monster (Diagram 2-16). The lead halfback now has the split end's man or the defender who has the deep third. This can be done from the twins set (Diagram 2-17) except the slot uses the normal stalk technique. The key coaching point in teaching the crack block is to insist that the end gets his head on the front side of the defender and blocks high above the waist. We also have him take one burst upfield before executing his crack block.

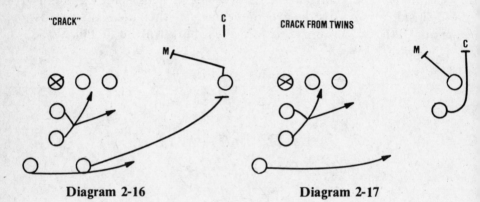

Diagram 2-16   Diagram 2-17

THE TED BLOCK

A TED block simply means a down block by the tight end on the first linebacker he comes to. This block is basica'' used in short yardage situations or if the secondary is over-shifted to the opposite end side and the tight end's blocking secondary is not needed (Diagram 2-18).

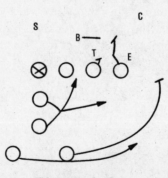

Diagram 2-18

THE HOOK BLOCK

A hook block is a block by the tight end on the end man on the line of scrimmage. Usually, this enables the tight end to block the defender who has the quarterback (Diagram 2-!9). This prevents an extreme move upfield by the defensive end to take the pitch, to prevent the defensive end from punishing the quarterback or to get the quarterback in the secondary on a short yardage play. It also is a good change of pace.

"HOOK"

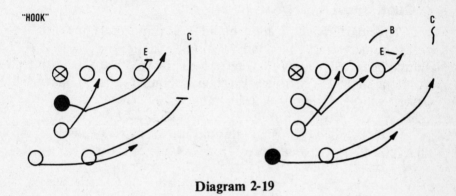

Diagram 2-19

BACKFIELD PLAY

The Multi-Bone Offense has two forms of triple options and two types of lead blocks. This gives the attack the flexibility to prevent the defense from dictating what it will allow.

One of the main differences between the "old Wishbone" and the Multi-Bone is that the Multi-Bone, with its two forms of triple options and its multiple blocking schemes both on the perimeter and in the line, prevents the defense from being the dictator. The Multi-Bone will not allow a defense to take away the pitch or take away the fullback. By remaining flexible, the offense eliminates defensive control. The Multi-Bone, by use of its variations in the triple option, actually enhances the total balance because any back can carry the ball.

However, if there is a situation of only one great back, these same variations can be used to feature the great back.

QUARTERBACK TECHNIQUES

The key to the success of the triple option is the play of the quarterback. With good technique and a good understanding of the attack, he can out-execute the best defense on the schedule. But before the quarterback can begin to learn the reads of the triple, he must completely master the physical mechanics. Only after these mechanics are perfected and the quarterback feels comfortable with them, will he be able to master the mental mechanics.

Quarterback's Steps

The quarterback's stance should be a comfortable one with his feet shoulder-width apart and his knees flexed slightly. The knees should be flexed to allow the quarterback to explode from the center upon the snap. The quarterback's hands should be placed under the center with his thumbs side by side and his fingers spread and relaxed.

After receiving the snap, the quarterback's first step is an open step at a 45 degree angle away from the line of scrimmage.

> **Coaching Point:** By stepping away from the line of scrimmage at a 45° angle the quarterback accomplishes four things:
>
> 1) He has moved away from the distraction of the blocking on the line of scrimmage which will allow him better concentration.
>
> 2) He has moved the mesh area into the backfield which eliminates the possibility of a defensive lineman getting his hand involved in the mesh. This eliminates a possible fumble in the mesh phase of the triple.
>
> 3) He has given himself a better angle to read the hand-off key.
>
> 4) He has given himself a better angle to approach the pitch key. He is moving to the pitch key "down hill" which enhances the play because the pitch key must make a quicker decision. Also, by approaching the pitch key at this angle, the quarterback actually improves his running ability because he will get upfield sooner if he keeps the ball. (Note: The difference between the paths of the Multi-Bone quarterback and the Splitback Veer quarterback (Diagram 2-20).

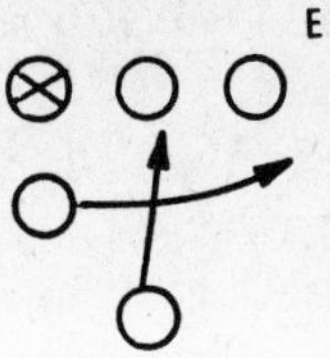

Diagram 2-20

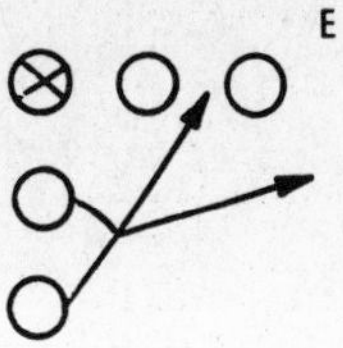

As the quarterback takes his initial step he simultaneously reaches back to the fullback with an almost stiff playside arm. He keeps the arm stiff until he makes his give or disconnect decision. Also, as the quarterback steps and reaches for fullback, his eyes must look to the hand-off key (the first man outside the offensive tackle).

If the hand-off is crashing down toward the fullback, the quarterback pulls the ball into his own numbers without meshing. The quarterback then positions the ball for a quick pitch as his eyes go directly to the pitch key.

If the hand-off key does anything else but crash, the quarterback places the ball in the fullback's hand-off pocket while still reading the hand-off key. By now the quarterback will take his second step, which is a catch-up step with his off-side leg. The quarterback should ride the fullback toward the line of scrimmage until he decides whether to give or keep. If the quarterback decides to keep, he pulls the ball into his own numbers and accelerates to the pitch key. If the quarterback decides to give the ball to the fullback, he removes the hand closest to the fullback from the ball and pushes the ball into the fullback's numbers with his other hand. After giving the ball to the fullback he must accelerate to the pitch key and fake a pitch.

> **Coaching Point:** The quarterback must make his decision before the ball reaches the hip that is closest to the line of scrimmage. He must *never* continue the mesh beyond this point.

The quicker the quarterback decides whether to give the ball or not, the better the play will be executed. The sooner the decision is made, then the sooner the fullback will know whether he is a blocker or a runner which will make him more effective at either. In the triple option the fullback is NEVER a faker. He is either a blocker or a runner. The days of tricking defenders with the triple option are long gone. Also, the sooner the decision, the faster the quarterback can get to the pitch key and either run or pitch. The speed of the play is dependent upon a quick decision by the quarterback. The final advantage of the quick read is the reduction in fumbles.

> *Note:* This style of meshplay is completely different from the original Wishbone concept of a long ride regardless of what the hand-off key did. The Multi-Bone concept is that it is better to have a wrong read than a long read. If the quarterback makes the wrong read, it is no gain. But if the quarterback and the fullback are tied up in a long mesh it could be a fumble. Also, the longer the mesh, the greater the chance of defensive pursuit catching up to the play.

The Quarterback's Multi-Reads

The quarterback has two different ways of reading the hand-off key. By giving him two ways of reading the hand-off key, his read can best fit the down and the distance situation. For example, in a third-and-one situation the give to the fullback would be more appropriate than the option phase of the triple. Conversely, in a third-and-six situation the option phase would have a better chance of getting the first down. The multiple reads get the coaching staff involved in the reading of the triple. The last advantage of multiple reads of the hand-off key is that it eliminates all area of doubt for the quarterback and makes it easier for him to make the quick read of the hand-off key that is so important to the quickness of the play.

THE DIVE READ

The hand-off read that is common to most triple option teams is the Multi-Bone Dive Read. The play is called "Dive and the blocking scheme"; for example, "Dive Veer," "Dive Zone" or "Dive X." This read of the triple option is used either in short yardage situations or to establish the fullback as a running threat.

The quarterback's thought process for the Dive Read is: "I will give the ball to the fullback every time unless I see the hand-off key make a sharp, direct move toward the fullback." In other words, when in doubt give to the fullback.

If the hand-off key is in a sit-and-read technique or if he is slow getting off the ball, the quarterback will give the ball to the fullback.

The fullback is expected to pick up three or four yards any time the hand-off key is not closing down hard on him. As stated earlier, this is a short yardage read.

The read has eliminated all doubt from the quarterback. The hand-off key can do one of three things (Diagram 2-21):

1) Move upfield or away from the fullback on a loop technique which will be a give to the fullback.

2) Play a sit-and-read technique which will also result in the fullback getting the ball.

3) Fire down hard on the fullback which is the only time the quarterback will *not* give the fullback the ball.

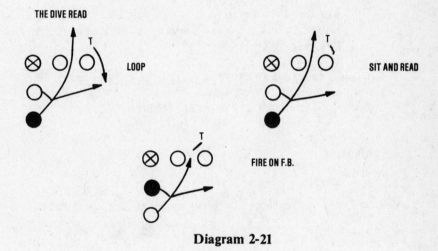

Diagram 2-21

THE OPTION READ

The read that is used most of the time in the Multi-Bone's triple option is the Option Read. The objective of the triple is to get the ball outside, and the option read increases the chances of the ball being pitched. The more the ball gets outside, the greater the chances of breaking big plays and producing points. The option read prevents the triple option from becoming a "three yards and a cloud of dust" play. It stretches the defensive front and makes it vulnerable.

The option read is called by saying "Option plus the blocking scheme"; for example, "Option Veer," "Option Zone" or "Option X."

The quarterback's thought process for the option read is "I will pull the ball every time unless I see the hand-off key make a direct move upfield or away from the fullback." In other words, when in doubt the quarterback pulls the ball.

If the hand-off key uses a sit-and-read technique when the option read is called, the quarterback will pull the ball and the fullback will attack the outside leg of the hand-off key.

The option read eliminates any indecision for the quarterback. The three reactions of the hand-off key are read as follows:

1) The hand-off key fires down on the fullback—the quarterback pulls the ball.

2) The hand-off key uses a sit-and-read technique—the quarterback pulls the ball.

3) The hand-off key moves either upfield or away from the fullback which is the only way the fullback would get the ball (Diagram 2-22).

Coaching Point: If the quarterback pulls the ball when he should have given to the fullback, he just follows the fullback upfield using him as a lead blocker (Diagram 2-22).

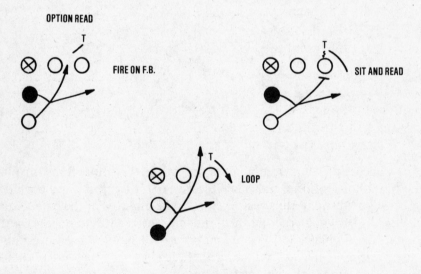

Diagram 2-22

Pitch Decision Rules

After reading the hand-off key, the quarterback explodes to the inside shoulder of the end man on the line of scrimmage, the pitch key. The quarterback does this whether he has the ball or not. If the quarterback has the ball, he must hold it with both hands at heart level as he approaches the pitch key.

The objective of the quarterback is to pitch the ball, so he must force the pitch key to play him. The angle of the quarterback approach is instrumental to this objective. By approaching the pitch key at the "down hill" angle and actually making the play look like a quarterback keep off-tackle, the quarterback can force the pitch key to commit himself. This technique is extremely important against a feathering defensive end. If the defensive end does not play the quarterback, the proper angle of approach and the quickness of the play can guarantee the quarterback at least four or more yards.

As the quarterback approaches the pitch key, he must be prepared for the following reactions:

1) a crashing defensive end;
2) a defensive end who fires upfield to pitch;
3) a reading defensive end;
4) a feathering end;
5) a cross charge between the defender responsible for pitch and the defender responsible for quarterback.

The quarterback's thought process for the pitch is "I will pitch the ball as soon as the pitch key's far shoulder turns toward me. If the pitch key fires upfield, I will keep only if there is no defender filling on me, or if the pitch key is unblocked."

This is how the quarterback should handle the situations he meets:

1) A crashing end—the quarterback must always expect a crashing end because he will have time to adjust to any other reaction. As soon as the quarterback pulls the ball from the fullback he should be prepared to pitch the ball. He must never attack a crashing end. The quarterback should just pitch the ball as soon as possible and protect himself (Diagram 2-23).

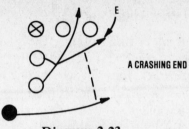

Diagram 2-23

2) A defensive end who fires upfield—the quarterback should look upfield to see if there is a defender filling on him (which is usually the case). If no one is taking the quarterback, he turns upfield and runs. If there is a defender filling on the quarterback, then he can pitch the ball because the lead blocker will block the defensive end (Diagram 2-24).

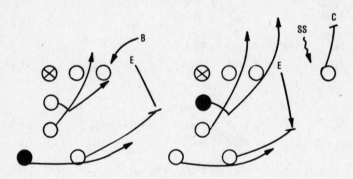

Diagram 2-24

3) A reading defensive end—the quarterback attacks the defensive end's inside shoulder until he shows his far shoulder. Then the quarterback pitches the ball. But if the defensive end has crossed his face, the quarterback keeps (Diagram 2-25).

4) A feathering defensive end—the feathering end tries to string out the play to buy time. The quarterback should keep attacking the feathering end's inside shoulder until he either commits to the quarterback or the end leaves too great a space between himself and the quarterback, in which case the quarterback runs. The angle of the quarterback's approach

A READING END

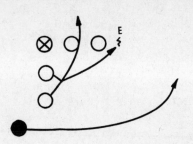

Diagram 2-25

A FEATHERING END

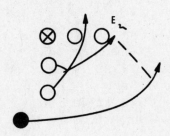

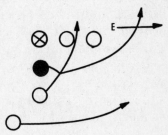

Diagram 2-26

PINCH

A CROSS CHARGE

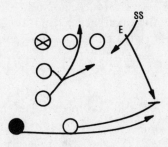

Diagram 2-27

and the speed of the play help defeat a feather end (Diagram 2-26).

5) A cross charge between the defender responsible for the pitch and the pitch key—the quarterback should recognize this possibility before the snap of the ball because this cross charge is easily recognizable. When the quarterback

approaches the pitch key and sees the stunt materialize, he pitches the ball because one defender will take him and the lead blocker will block the other (Diagram 2-27).

Coaching Point: The quarterback should *not* pitch the ball once he crosses the line of scrimmage. Once he decides to keep he becomes a runner and must make the play work. This rule eliminates indecision or hesitation on the part of the quarterback.

The Pitch Technique

The pitch technique is very simple. The quarterback extends his arm from his heart while he steps in the direction of the trailing halfback and rotates his hand with his thumb turning down under the ball. This action will cause the ball to tumble end over end and will get to the back as quickly as possible. The pitch should have some velocity and *not* be just a lob pitch. The quarterback should also look directly at the trailing halfback and aim the pitch at the trailing halfback's heart. (This is a heart-to-heart pitch because it travels from the quarterback's heart to the halfback's heart).

Coaching Point: The quarterback should never pitch the ball low. He must always aim for the pitch man's heart. The biggest cause of fumbles on the pitch is a low pitch that is hard to handle. The quarterback should also look at the pitch man. The position of the halfback behind the guards has eliminated the need for the blind pitch. The blind pitch was popular in the old Split T in which the backs were positioned behind the tackles (Diagram 2-28).

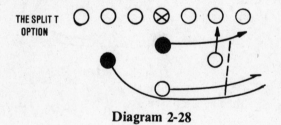

Diagram 2-28

FULLBACK PLAY IN THE MULTI-BONE TRIPLE OPTION

The fullback is important to the initial phase of the triple option. He must average at least four yards per carry and be able to constantly pick up tough yards. The fullback must also be a dedicated blocker. He is always either a runner or a blocker, but *never* a faker. The fullback's rules differ slightly according to the blocking scheme used, but his steps are always constant. If the fullback gets the ball, his rule is: "rumble, stumble, but never fumble."

The fullbacks steps are as follows:

1) On the snap of the ball, the fullback takes a lead step in the direction of the play and gets his offside arm up high under his chin to form a large pocket in which the quarterback can place the ball.

2) The fullback then explodes to the outside hip of the guard with his head up and his eyes open.

3) The fullback reads what is happening in the guard-tackle gap and reacts depending on the blocking scheme used and the defensive reaction.

Fullback Play with Veer Blocking

In veer blocking the fullback's rule is to get outside the block of the tackle, whether or not he is getting the ball. No matter what happens, he must get outside the block of the tackle.

If the fullback gets the ball, he carries it with both hands and gets outside the first defender looking to bust the play. He must *never* be tackled with an arm tackle, and he must break at least one tackle every time he carries the ball.

If he does not get the ball, the fullback must attack the outside knee of the first defender outside the tackle's block. If the fullback hits the guard-tackle gap and sees a pinching tackle, then he must

FULLBACK VEER BLOCKING

"PINCH"   READ TACKLE   EAGLE

Diagram 2-29

block the scraping linebacker. If he sees a tackle in a sit-and-read technique, the fullback attacks the tackle's outside knee. If the fullback sees an eagle front, he treats it as a pinching tackle and blocks the linebacker (Diagram 2-29). The fullback must always keep moving, getting width as he goes and must never let a defender cross his face.

Fullback Play with Zone Blocking

In zone blocking, the fullback will approach the guard-tackle gap exactly as he does in veer blocking, but his execution is not the same.

If the fullback gets the ball, he reads the block of the guard and cuts off that block.

If the ball is pulled, the fullback attacks the outside leg of the first man he sees from the guard-tackle gap outside. The fullback could double with the guard and block: 1) a pinching tackle, 2) an Eagle tackle, 3) a tackle in an even front. However, the fullback must also be prepared to block a tackle playing the sit-and-read technique without help from the guard. (Diagram 2-30).

FULLBACK ZONE BLOCKING

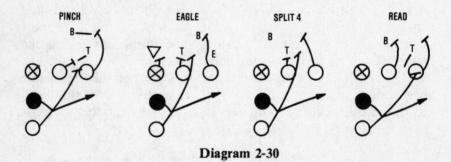

Diagram 2-30

Coaching Point: If the fullback is double teaming with the guard and cannot see the outside leg of the defender, he continues down field.

Fullback Play with "X" Blocking

In the "X" blocking scheme, the fullback gets the outside hip of the guard and follows him through the hole. If the fullback is getting the ball, he breaks off the guard's block. If the ball is pulled from the fullback, he continues downfield and blocks the first defender that crosses his face (Diagram 2-31).

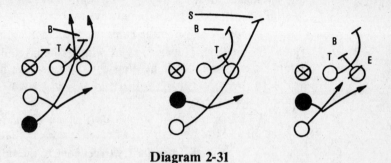

Diagram 2-31

> **Coaching Point:** Most of the time with "X" blocking, when the fullback does not get the ball, he will be tackled by the first man outside the guard's block.

HALFBACK PLAY IN THE MULTI-BONE TRIPLE OPTION

The halfback in the Multi-Bone triple option is either a pitch man or a blocker. There is not a tailback or a blocking back. Both halfbacks must block for each other, which creates a great team spirit. The halfbacks must stretch the defense laterally with their speed and execution at the perimeter.

The Halfback As Pitch Man

The offside halfback is pitch man (except in broken bone sets). His steps are as follows:

1) As the ball is snapped, the halfback takes an open lead step parallel to the line of scrimmage and simultaneously pivots his hips and shoulders so they are parallel to the sidelines. This step establishes his path.

2) As soon as the ball is snapped, the pitch man should look for the pitch.

3) After his initial step, the pitch man must get on a five-yard highway to the sidelines staying on the outside hip of the lead blocker. The halfback is told to get on the five-yard highway to gain width and prevent him from turning upfield too soon.

4) He must always stay on the lead blocker's outside hip. His rule is "out-side hip, never dip." This sets up the onside halfback's lead block.

5) The pitch man must always catch the ball above all else. He must always expect a pitch and always look for a bad pitch.

6) Once he catches the pitch, he can read the blocking.

7) The pitch man must always go as wide as he possibly can before turning upfield. If he aims for the sidelines, he can stretch the defense, run away from pursuit and open a large running lane.

8) The ball carrier can turn upfield *only* when the defender responsible for the pitch crosses the lead blocker's face.

9) If he does turn upfield, he must try to get back to the sidelines as soon as possible. Actually, his "turn" upfield is a "dip" upfield (Diagram 2-32).

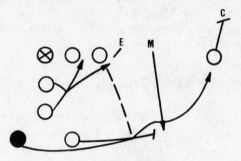

Diagram 2-32

10) When the pitch man does turn upfield he must look for the receiver's stalk block and get yardage.

THE WHIRLEY STEP

The only other move the halfback must make when he is pitch man is to take a whirley step. When in a broken bone set and the triple is run to the same side that the half-back is lined up, he must take a whirley step (Diagram 2-33). The whirley step is executed as follows:

1) a lead step with the halfback's inside foot;

2) a catch-up step with the outside foot;

3) a pivot off the lead foot;
4) a sprint on the pitch highway.

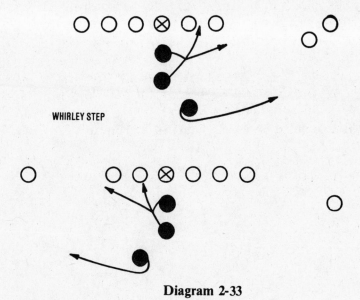

Diagram 2-33

The Halfback Blocking

The halfbacks have two blocking schemes for the triple option. The lead block is the normal blocking scheme that is used. This is the scheme in which the lead blocker blocks the defender assigned to pitch. This scheme is always run unless "load" is called. Load blocking is the scheme used to block the defender assigned to the quarterback.

THE LEAD BLOCK

Picking out whom to block is extremely important and is carefully explained. As the halfback comes out of his stance, he aims for the second defender from the sidelines. He is usually the defender assigned to the pitch. From this point he follows the path theory and stays on his path regardless of what the defender does. If the defender disappears, the lead blocker *never* chases him but assumes someone else will be replacing him as the pitch defender. There is never the need to chase someone to block because the ball carrier is on his outside hip, so the defenders are going to have to come to the blocker.

As in all blocking situations, the blocker must be prepared for all possible situations he might see. The halfback might have to block (Diagram 2-34):

1) an inverted monster;
2) a rotating corner;
3) a firing defensive end;
4) an outside linebacker;
5) an outside backer or end in a goal line defense (Diagram 2-34).

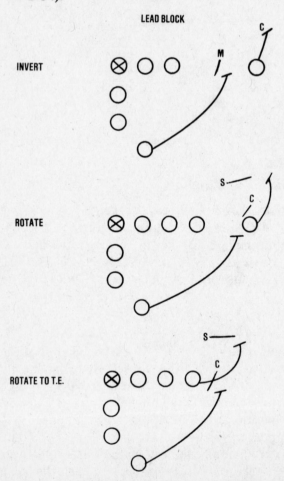

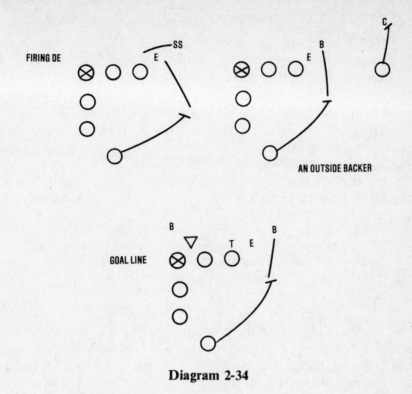

Diagram 2-34

Blocking an inverted monster presents no problem in recognition, but the lead blocker must be aware of a monster that fires upfield.

The rotating corner requires an adjustment because the corner is technically the first defender from the sidelines. But by aiming for the second man from the sidelines the lead blocker will have more than enough time to adjust. Rotation is easily recognizable by the depths of the defenders. It should be expected when the triple is run to the tight end side.

The firing defensive end is another stunt that is easily recognizable prior to the snap. There is usually a defender close to the defensive end to take the quarterback. Once the lead back spots the pitch defender, he aims for him. If the defensive end takes the pitch, the lead back will be in position to block him. This technique can also be used to recognize the pitch defender in a Split Four or goal line defense.

LEAD BLOCK TECHNIQUE

The closeness of the ball carrier and blocker is one of the great advantages of the full bone. It is not likely a defender will beat the blocker and still have the time to make the tackle. The position of the two backs also makes the blocking technique extremely easy because the defender must come through the blocker.

Once the lead blocker picks out the pitch defender, he aims his inside shoulder at the defender's outside knee. Upon reaching the defender, the lead blocker punches his inside arm through his outside knee and runs through the defender's outside leg. The lead blocker must *always* make a collision and *never* leave his feet.

> **Coaching Point:** The lead blocker must always try to get outside position. But should the pitch defender cross his face, he should drive the defender into the sidelines to create a large running lane for the ball carrier (Diagram 2-32).

THE LOAD BLOCK

Recognizing the defender assigned to the quarterback is the first step of the load block. When load blocking, the halfback picks out the third defender from the sidelines (usually a defensive end) and follows the path theory. if the defender disappears, don't chase him. Someone will be replacing him.

The load blocking halfback must be prepared to block:

1) a crashing defensive end;
2) a safety inverting on the quarterback;
3) a crashing cornerback to the tight end side;
4) a cross charging outside linebacker in a Split Four;
5) an eagle linebacker (Diagram 2-35).

Blocking a crashing defensive end is the easiest load block because the defensive end usually doesn't see it coming. The key to blocking the inverting safety, cross charging backer or an eagle backer is to stay on course under control and keep alert. These cross charge stunts are easily recognizable prior to the snap.

THE LOAD BLOCK TECHNIQUE

Load blocking technique differs slightly from lead blocking. When using a load block the halfback aims for the defender's hip

THE LOAD BLOCK

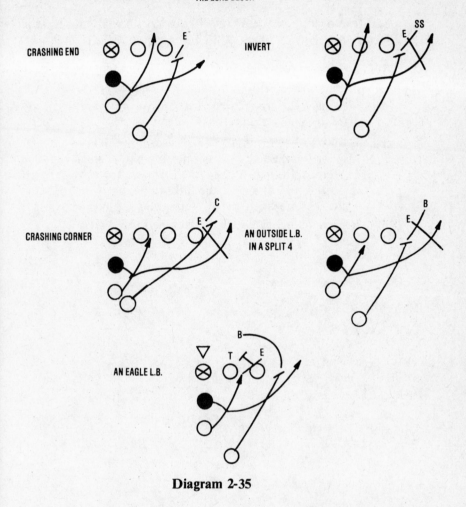

CRASHING END

INVERT

CRASHING CORNER

AN OUTSIDE L.B.
IN A SPLIT 4

AN EAGLE L.B.

Diagram 2-35

because he is not looking to cut the defender. If the halfback cut the defender, it would create a pile of bodies, usually on the line of scrimmage. Instead, the load blocker wants to drive the defender and that is why his aiming point is higher. Also, by aiming higher, the defender cannot reach over the top of the block to grab the quarterback. In lead blocking, the possibility of a defender reaching over the lead blocker is not likely because the ball carrier has much more running room than the quarterback on the line of scrimmage.

WHY LOAD BLOCK?

In addition to load blocking to add diversity and flexibility, the other reasons for the use of the load block are:

1) It helps protect the quarterback from crashing ends.

2) It makes the inverting safety move unsound.

3) It handles the cross charge between the outside backer and defensive end very nicely.

4) It is very effective in a short yardage situation.

5) In poor weather conditions when pitching the ball could be dangerous, the load block is the sensible alternative. *Note:* It is another advantage of the full Multi-Bone over the strict Splitback offense or the "I" formation.

6) It prevents the defense from "taking Q.B."

CHAPTER 3

The Multi-Bone Power Attack

The triple option, though very effective, is a finesse play which depends on execution of reads. But to have a multiple offense, a power attack is also needed. There are a number of other advantages to installing a few basic plays to knock people off the ball rather than finesse them. The following list is why the power attack was added to the Multi-Bone:

1) It provides a great short yardage attack.
2) Running power with the triple option provides a great change of pace and it takes advantage of a defensive tackle using a sit-and-read technique.
3) It takes advantage of a "feather" end.
4) The power attack is an all-weather attack.
5) It is good to have when on either your opponent's goal line or your own.
6) A defense can not sit back off the ball against a power game.
7) If the opponent is physically weaker, the power attack can be tough to defend.
8) It is a good way to give the ball to a superior back.
9) The power attack also provides relief for the quarterback mentally and physically because he just fakes and hands-off in this phase of the attack.
10) It is a good attack to use if there is an inexperienced quarterback at the helm.

Having a three-back backfield is one of the big advantages of the Multi-Bone over the Splitback Veer set. The Multi-Bone can provide all the power of the Power I attack.

THE BELLY PLAY

The belly is the most important and effective of the power plays. It can be an entire offense in itself because like the triple option it can attack three areas. It can be run with the fullback carrying on a dive, the quarterback running around the end, or the halfback carrying on an off-tackle play. Borrowed from Bobby Dodd's inside belly series that he ran at Georgia Tech, the belly is a great complement to the triple option because it takes advantage of a tackle who is agressively taking the fullback. It is the best short yardage play in football because the action of the diving fullback forces the defensive tackle to take him. He cannot risk gambling that the fullback does not have the ball. The belly also takes advantage of an end who is soft playing the option or is firing upfield on a pitch. The belly also provides a way to give the ball to a good halfback, with a lead blocker off-tackle. This is the basis of the Power I attack.

The Backfield Action of the Belly

The quarterback's steps for the belly are similar to his steps for the triple option. He open steps on a 45° angle and gets the ball into the fullback's pocket exactly as he does in the triple option (see Quarterback Steps in the Triple Option). The only difference is that after the ball is in the fullback's pouch, the quarterback gives a ride to his front hip before he pulls the ball from the fullback (or gives to him on the fullback belly). Once the quarterback has meshed, he hands the ball off as deep as he can to the offside halfback to give the halfback running room. He then sprints around the end. If the play is the quarterback belly, the quarterback fakes the ball to the off halfback and sprints to the sidelines (Diagram 3-1).

THE FULLBACK BELLY

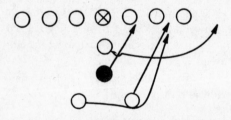

Diagram 3-1

THE QUARTERBACK BELLY

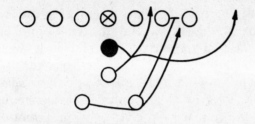

THE BELLY

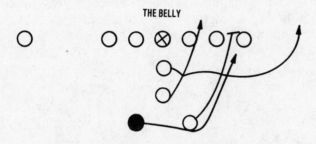

Diagram 3-1 (continued)

THE FULLBACK STEPS

The fullback aims for the outside leg of the guard just as he does in the triple option. His rules are exactly the same as in the triple option. Once the ball is pulled he looks for someone to block. The only difference is that he knows when he is getting the ball before the snap. When the fullback belly is run he reads the block of the guard. The fullback must always dent the line of scrimmage whether he has the ball or not.

THE LEAD BLOCKER'S STEPS

The lead blocker in the belly play will determine exactly where the running back will go. His rule is to read the block of the tackle and to block accordingly. If the offensive tackle blocks down, the lead blocker cuts outside, upfield and looks for the backer. If the offensive tackle blocks out, the lead blocker breaks back inside and blocks as though it were an isolation play.

The only exception occurs when the TED block is used. Then the lead halfback runs a load block just as though it were a load call on the triple option.

THE RUNNING BACK'S ROUTE

The running back lead-steps parallel to the line of scrimmage exactly as he would when he runs the triple option. However, when he reaches the point where the lead blocker was aligned, he bursts upfield following the course of the lead blocker. If there is no lead blocker, he follows the block of the offensive tackle.

Once he turns upfield, the running back opens up his inside arm (exactly as the fullback does in the triple option) and awaits the hand-off.

After receiving the hand-off, he follows the lead blocker and runs to daylight. He must go north and south with his shoulder pads parallel to the line of scrimmage and gain positive yardage (Diagram 3-2).

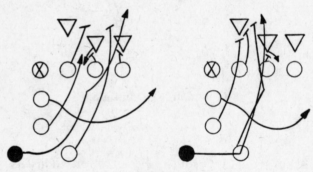

Diagram 3-2

Line Blocking for the Belly Play

In keeping with the multiple philosophy, five blocking schemes are used for the belly. Rather than give up on a play, a change in the blocking scheme might make the play go.

Two blocking schemes used for the belly play are exactly the same as used for the triple option: Zone and Veer. Zone blocking is used because the belly play can be run without a lead blocker with this scheme. If the defensive tackle comes down, he is double teamed by the guard and the fullback. The tackle picks up the linebacker. If the defensive tackle takes a wide charge, the offensive tackle blocks him out and the play will go over the guard, with the guard and the fullback on the linebacker. (The actual techniques are described in Chapter 2.) The tight end seals inside and then turns the defensive end out (Diagram 3-3).

Diagram 3-3

If the defensive tackle is constantly taking the fullback or if the nose guard is extremely troublesome, veer blocking is the answer. The line follows the same rules as they would for the triple option (Chapter 2). The lead blocker blocks the linebacker if the defensive tackle plays the fullback. Or he will attack the defensive tackle if he does not play the fullback. The lead blocker should attack the defensive tackle's outside hip but he takes him any way he can (Diagram 3-4).

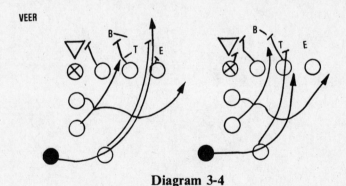

Diagram 3-4

The most common scheme used for the belly is base blocking. This is the oldest blocking scheme in the book. The rule is: "inside gap, on, over, outside gap." The guard aims for the outside hip of the first defender on or off the line of scrimmage from his inside gap to his outside gap. The onside tackle does likewise but can take the defender any way he wants to go because the lead blocker will adjust accordingly. By having a lead block, stunts do not present a problem (Diagram 3-5).

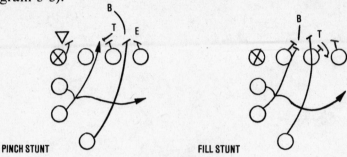

PINCH STUNT   FILL STUNT

Diagram 3-5

The first variation of the base scheme is TED blocking. This is the same as base blocking except for the tight end and the lead blocker. Instead of turning the defensive end out, the tight end executes a TED block (see Chapter 2), and the lead blocker executes a load block on the first man outside the tight end's block. The ball carrier reads the lead blocker's block and runs to daylight. This is an effective short yardage scheme because the TED block causes the defensive end to close down and sets up the load block (Diagram 3-6).

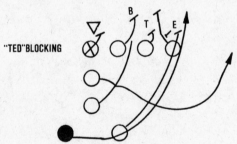

"TED" BLOCKING

Diagram 3-6

The final scheme has been borrowed from the Delaware Wing T and is called "On-Trap." The name is derived from the fact that the onside guard is the trapper. The tackle and tight end TED block. The onside guard pulls and kicks out the first man outside the tight end's block, and the fullback fills for the pulling guard (Diagram 3-7).

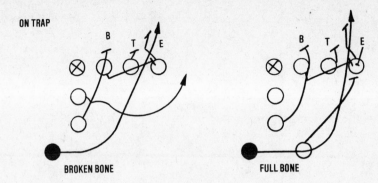

Diagram 3-7

The pulling guard's technique is the same as the technique used in "X" blocking (see Chapter 2) except with this scheme he blocks the inside shoulder of the defensive end.

Though this scheme can be run from a broken bone, the lead blocker from a full bone can really set up a trap block. The lead blocker approaches the defensive end as though it was a load block and then by-passes him and blocks a defensive back. But by faking a load block, the lead blocker will distract the defensive end and force him to play the load block. The defensive end will be a sitting duck for the trapping guard.

BASE BLOCKING TECHNIQUE

Base blocking technique for the onside guard and tackle are exactly the same. They each fire their inside shoulder to the outside breastplate of the defender over them. The onside guard and tackle then drive the defender wherever he wants to go.

The only exception is when the fullback belly is called. The guard blocks according to zone rules (Chapter 2). If the defensive tackle pinches down, the guard blocks him. If the defensive tackle does anything else, he fires at the linebacker. The onside tackle aims his outside shoulder to the inside breastplate of the defender over him and fights for inside position. This blocking adjustment eliminates the scrape stunt (Diagram 3-8).

The offside technique is the same as the offside line technique for the triple option (Chapter 2). The Multi-Bone offside line technique always remains the same regardless of play or blocking scheme.

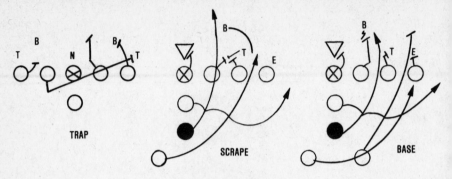

Diagram 3-8

THE FULLBACK DIVE

The second play in the power attack is the fullback dive. It is not a fancy play, but it can be a valuable addition to an offense. The following are the five main reasons for having a fullback dive in the Multi-Bone offense:

1) It provides another way of attacking the hand-off key.
2) The fullback dive devastates a hand-off key that is playing a sit-and-read style of play.
3) A superior fullback can be used regardless of defensive option responsibility.
4) The fullback dive fits nicely with the triple option. It is the triple option with base blocking and a predetermined give to the fullback.
5) It is a great short yardage call.

The same backfield action as the triple option is used. The only difference is that the fullback knows he is definitely getting the ball.

The base blocking scheme is the same scheme used for the fullback belly play. The fullback reads the blocking and runs to daylight (Diagram 3-9).

Wedge blocking is also used for the dive. Wedge blocking means that each lineman steps down to his inside and drives his shoulder into the back of the next offensive lineman inside him. The guard to the side called is always the point of the wedge. For example, wedge right would mean the right guard is the point of the wedge. The key to wedge blocking is for the offensive line to keep driving their legs and literally wedge the defensive line downfield (Diagram 3-10).

This may be one of the oldest plays in football but still effective.

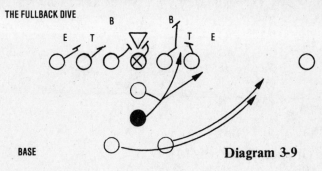

THE FULLBACK DIVE

BASE

Diagram 3-9

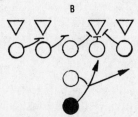

FULLBACK WEDGE

Diagram 3-10

THE SWEEP

The outside power play of the Multi-Bone is the Sweep borrowed from John McKay. Many coaches feel there is no need for a sweep in an option attack because you have an outside play with the option. But the sweep is effective and necessary for several reasons:

1) It provides an alternate way of getting outside.
2) It is a sure way of getting the ball to the halfbacks running wide with lead blockers.
3) It is a great complement ot the triple option because it takes advantage of a feathering or crashing end (two of the most common defensive techniques against the triple option).
4) It allows an offense to attack a defense away from the

monster with power. *Note:* Because the triple option is so effective to the wide side of the field, defenses will play their monster there. The sweep can attack the short side of the field (to the tight end) with power away from their monster. Wouldn't Power I or Wing T teams love to be able to do that? This is another advantage of the three-backs backfield.

5) The sweep is a great power complement to the belly. If defenses are stacked against the belly by playing the defensive end head up or inside to the tight end, it is sensible to go to the sweep.

Backfield Action

THE QUARTERBACK STEPS

The sweep provides an opportunity to rest the quarterback. After receiving the snap from center the quarterback reverse pivots. Then he makes a low two-handed lob pitch to the waist of the off-side halfback. After pitching the ball, the quarterback continues down the line of scrimmage to prevent penetration.

THE FULLBACK AND THE ONSIDE BLOCKING RULES

The fullback blocks the first man outside the tight end's block. To the split end side he blocks the first man outside the tackle's block. The fullback stays on his path at all times and blocks the first person to cross his face. For example, if the defensive end to the split end side fires upfield, the fullback *does not* chase him but continues on his path looking for someone to cross it. If the man is across his face once he turns upfield, the fullback drives him into the sidelines. If the defender on the tight end is escaping the tight end's block, he cuts the outside knee of the defender.

The onside halfback blocks the first man outside the fullback's block. He is blocking the widest man in the defense to the tight end side and the man responsible for pitch to the split end side. The halfback must stay on his path just as he would in the triple option (Diagram 3-11).

To the split end side, a crack block can be run. This is the same as the triple option blocking (Diagram 3-12). To the tight end side, the tight end can be blocked down which is exactly the same blocking as in the belly (Diagram 3-13). By TED blocking, there is a tendency for the defensive end to close down, thus setting up the fullback's block.

SWEEP BLOCKING

TO TIGHT END

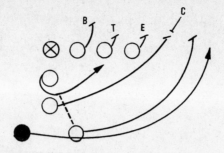

TO SPLIT END

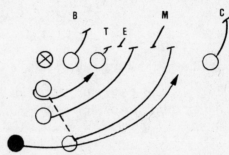

VS FIRING DE

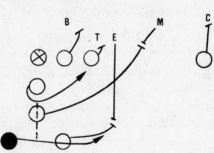

Diagram 3-11

CRACK

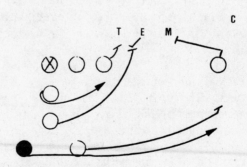

Diagram 3-12

TEO

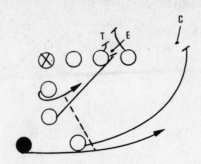

Diagram 3-13

Backfield Blocking Technique

The blocking technique for the lead back and the fullback are exactly the same techniques taught to the lead blocker in the triple option (see Chapter 2). It is to attack the outside knee of the defender.

OFFSIDE HALFBACK STEPS

The offside halfback is the ball carrier in the sweep and follows the same path he does for the triple option. He gets on the outside hip of the lead halfback and turns upfield only if a defender crosses the lead blocker's face. The ball carrier must look for the pitch immediately after the ball is snapped, then run exactly as he does in the triple option.

Line Blocking

Line blocking is base blocking with the tight end hook blocking the end man on the line of scrimmage. An alternate blocking scheme is to block the tight end down just as he does in the belly play or triple option.

Coaching Points:
1) The offensive tackle in blocking base must hook his man also by aiming for his outside breast and working for outside position.
2) Against a Split Four, the veer blocking and base blocking are the same with the tight end blocking down (Diagram 3-14).

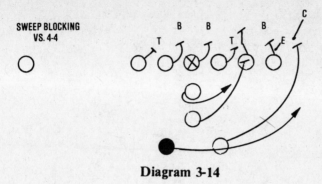

Diagram 3-14

Incorporating a sweep play in the Multi-Bone involves very little teaching:

1) The receivers have the same blocking as they have in the triple option.
2) The running back takes the same course as he does in the triple option.
3) The line blocking is the base scheme.
4) The lead blocker uses the same lead blocking technique as used in the triple option.

QUARTERBACK SNEAK

The oldest play in football is the quarterback sneak. Probably every team in the country does it the same way. Wedge blocking is used, and the quarterback burrows down into the line. The only difference is that we run it off any play action. For example, the

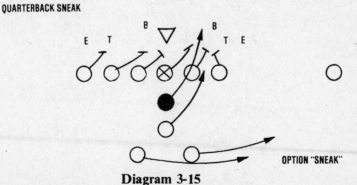

Diagram 3-15

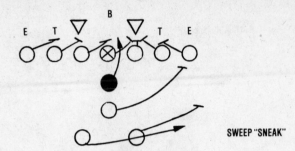

Diagram 3-15 (continued)

quarterback might call triple option right quarterback sneak or sweep right quarterback sneak (Diagram 3-15).

CHAPTER **4**

The Multi-Bone Counter Attack

For any offense to be complete, a counter attack is an absolute must. The counter attack is needed for the Multi-Bone offense for several reasons:

1) To threaten the entire width of the field from the same initial action as the triple option.
2) To slow down backside pursuit. To maintain the numbers advantage of the triple option, it is necessary to control or threaten backside defenders.
3) To attack an exceptionally quick defense by using their quickness against them. Over-pursuit can be a great offensive weapon.
4) To get better blocking angles on big, strong opponents.
5) To destroy a defense's initial keys.
6) To force a defense to think rather than react.
7) To insure that a good fullback or halfback carries the ball regardless of defensive assignment.
8) To provide another style of attack.

The counter attack adds the misdirection of the Delaware Wing T as the power attack added the best of the Power I formation. The counter attack has enough flexibility to use it the entire game if a defense refuses to play us honestly or persists in its own pursuit patterns.

INSIDE COUNTER ATTACK

The inside counter attack is designed to attack the nose guard, backside linebacker and backside defensive tackle. It also provides another way of running between the tackles other than the power attack and triple option. A defense must never be allowed to take away the inside attack by just pinching their tackles. The inside counters force the defense to commit four or five defenders to stop the interior running attack. If the inside counters never gain a yard but occupy four or five defenders, they have done their job. By keeping track of who is making the tackles on the triple option, it is simple to exploit that defender. If the troublesome defender is the nose guard, backside tackle, or one of the inside linebackers, then the inside counters are the answer.

Inside Counter Attack Line Blocking

The line blocking for the inside counters is exactly the same for all four counters. As with the other phases of the Multi-Bone Attack, more than one blocking scheme is used. An offense that relies on only one blocking scheme for each play will be in big trouble against a team of equal ability. When there are four blocking variations for the inside counters, a defense cannot read the play with any consistency.

BASE BLOCKING

Base blocking is the same scheme that was used in the power attack except both offensive tackles aim their outside shoulders at the inside knees of the defenders over them. By taking this aiming point, the tackles can seal the inside running lane. This creates an area where the ball carrier can read the blocks of the center and the guards. Both guards aim their outside shoulders at the inside knees of the defenders over them. The center takes the defender over him any way he can. As long as the center stays with the block, the ball carrier will run to daylight (Diagram 4-1).

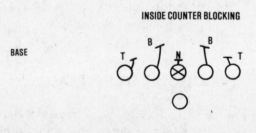

Diagram 4-1

WEDGE BLOCKING

The wedge blocking scheme has come from the power attack. The first down lineman to the playside of the line of scrimmage is wedged. For example: against an odd front, the nose guard is wedged, and against an even front, the defender over the guard is wedged. Though this scheme is basically a short yardage adjustment, it is helpful against a very quick nose guard. It can also be used if a defense is constantly pinching their tackles (Diagram 4-2).

WEDGE

Diagram 4-2

FOLD BLOCKING

The first blocking scheme unique to the counter attack is fold blocking. This blocking variation is extremely effective against a slanting or pinching defense. Fold blocking is the solution for blocking a physically superior defensive line because it provides blocking angles. Fold blocking is also an excellent change of pace.

The playside lineman who is covered makes the call. If he does not think he can base block the defender playing over him, he calls fold blocking. He may call "fold" because the defender is playing an inside shade on him or because he is just too strong to base block. If the defense has been pinching or slanting their tackles, the counter will be sent to the quarterback with fold blocking included. Fold blocking can be executed by either the playside tackle and guard or the playside guard and center (Diagram 4-3).

FOLD

Diagram 4-3

FOLD BLOCKING TECHNIQUE

The technique for fold blocking is exactly opposite the "x" blocking technique. The uncovered lineman steps out to the first playside shoulder into the near breastplate of the down man and works to maintain good body position. From this point the uncovered lineman executes a drive block. A stalemate is all that is needed with this block. If the defensive lineman is pinching, this block should stop his charge and create a stalemate situation.

The step-around man is the covered lineman. His technique is the same as the step-around technique of "x" blocking except the step-around is toward the center. He whips his inside arm back and takes a lead step parallel to the line of scrimmage. Then he lets the inside offensive lineman pass and turns upfield right off his tail. He aims his inside shoulder for the near breastplate of the first unblocked defender he sees. The block should be above the waist, so there is no danger of the defender going over the block. Also by making a high block, the lineman actually hides the ball carrier.

TRAP BLOCKING

The final scheme for the inside counter attack is trap blocking. This blocking scheme comes directly from the Delaware Wing T attack. It can turn any of the four inside counters into a trap play. This scheme is reserved mainly for odd fronts because the other three schemes work more effectively against even fronts. Trap blocking is used if a nose guard is too tough to handle without a combo block on him.

The playside linemen block as though it was Veer blocking. The playside guard and center combo block the nose guard and backside linebacker. The playside tackle comes through the inside knee of the defender over him and blocks the onside linebacker. The misdirection in the backfield really enhances the blocking angles in this scheme.

The offside guard whips his playside arm back, opens his hips, stays low, and pulls directly off the playside tackle's tail. He blocks the first defender outside the tackle's block. The "downhill" approach by the guard makes this block easy to execute. If the defensive tackle is closing down, the guard can get good body position on him. The trapper aims his playside shoulder for the defender's near breastplate and executes a "running drive block." Once contact is made, he must slide his head upfield to stay between the defender and the ball carrier. This is basically the same technique used for the "On trap" described in Chapter 3 (Diagram 4-4).

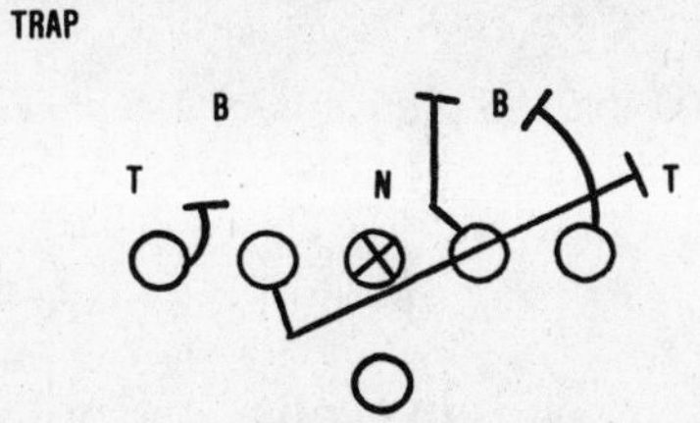

TRAP

Diagram 4-4

Backfield Actions

The Multi-Bone inside counter game has four different backfield actions that can be used with any of the blocking schemes to provide a very diversified attack.

THE FULLBACK COUNTER

The fullback counter is a simple counter but can devastate a defense with an over-active nose guard. This play is also very effective against a team that is trying to stop the fullback with pinching tackles. The fullback counter is a sure way to get the ball to a good fullback regardless of defensive responsibility (Diagram 4-5).

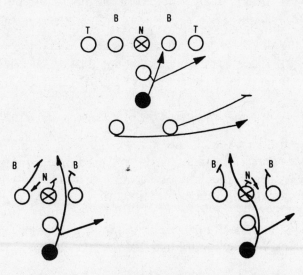

THE FULLBACK COUNTER

Diagram 4-5

The halfbacks run the same paths they run for the triple option.

The quarterback open steps at a 90 degree angle. This step accomplishes two things:

1) It gets the ball to the fullback deeper in the backfield, which allows him to read the blocking and;

2) It moves the quarterback farther away from the line of scrimmage to give the fullback more room to make his cut.

The quarterback then hands the ball to the fullback and accelerates to the defensive end. This acceleration will provide most of the deception of the play.

The fullback's course is slightly tighter than his triple option route. The fullback aims for the inside leg of the guard and reads the guard-center gap. He either runs through the gap or, if it is clogged, he cuts off the center's block. Most likely the fullback will break back against the grain. The fullback's shoulders should always remain parallel to the line of scrimmage, and he should always look for positive yardage.

This is a quick-hitting counter that will guarantee that the fullback will never be "taken away" by the defense.

THE HALFBACK COUNTER

The importance of the halfback counter in the Multi-Bone Attack can never be overlooked. This play must be run for the following reasons:

1) It takes advantage of a team that is keying the fullback.

2) It exploits a defense with a middle linebacker.

3) It enables the halfbacks to get the ball running north and south.

4) It threatens a fast-flowing defense.

The fullback's steps are exactly the same as his steps in the fullback counter. This play requires a good fake from the fullback. He must "dent" the line of scrimmage and run with reckless abandon. In short yardage situations the fullback actually "jumps" over the line of scrimmage.

The quarterback open-steps at a 90 degree angle (as he does in the fullback counter) and flash fakes to the fullback.

Coaching Point: The quarterback must never risk a fumble by placing the ball in the fullback's belly. The action of the fullback diving into the line and the quarterback flashing the ball in his direction provides a more than adequate fake.

After the fake, the quarterback continues to pivot and hands the ball to the halfback as deep as possible in the backfield. He then retreats straight back to fake a pass.

Coaching Point: The halfback should get the ball deep in the backfield to give him more time to read the blocks.

The offside halfback does what he would do in the triple option. He takes off just as though he was going to make the lead block for the triple option.

The ball-carrying halfback jab steps upfield at a 45 degree angle with his inside foot. Then he drives off his front foot toward the line of scrimmage. As he explodes to the line of scrimmage, his inside arm should come up under his chin forming a large hand-off pocket. Once the halfback gets the ball, he reads the butt of the guard and runs to daylight. Again the ball carrier's shoulders should be parallel to the line of scrimmage and he should be looking for positive yardage (Diagram 4-6).

THE HALFBACK COUNTER

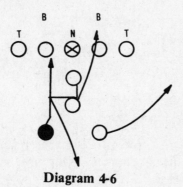

Diagram 4-6

THE QUARTERBACK COUNTER

The quickest-hitting and easiest to run of all the Multi-Bone counters is the quarterback counter. Though simple, it is needed because:

1) It destroys all halfback and fullback keys.

2) It allows the quarterback to carry the ball on a counter type of play.

3) Its quickness exploits a slanting nose guard.

4) It involves no ball handling, thus is a great rainy day play.

5) It prevents a defense from "taking away" the quarterback as a running threat.

6) It allows a quarterback with limited running ability to be a threat to run.

The fullback and halfbcks follow their triple option paths. The fullback again must "dent" the line of scrimmage.

The quarterback starts the play just as though it was the triple option. But after faking to the fullback, he looks back and reads the center's block. The key to this play is patience. The quarterback cannot rush the play. He must allow time for pursuit to develop before running at the center's block (Diagram 4-7).

QUARTERBACK COUNTER

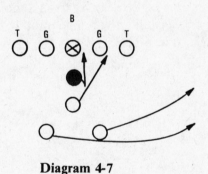

Diagram 4-7

THE HALFBACK SCISSORS

The final play of the inside counter series is the halfback scissors. Though this play requires a bit more practice time than the other counters, it is needed because:

1) It allows all four backs to have a counter. This is a lead back counter while the halfback counter was a pitchback counter.

2) It is another way of getting the ball to the halfbacks.

3) It destroys a defense that keys fullback and offside halfback.

The fullback and offside halfback use the same routes as they would in the triple option. The fullback must "dent" the line of scrimmage to draw defenders to him.

The quarterback's initial steps are the same as his triple option steps. After the fake to the fullback, he reaches back away from the line of scrimmage with his playside arm. The quarterback then *looks* to the onside halfback and hands the ball off. He then accelerates to the defensive end.

The ball-carrying halfback takes three steps toward the defensive end. This should appear to be the start of a load block. His steps should be: 1) a lead step 2) a crossover step and 3) a final step that he plants, and pivots off. After his third step, he brings his outside arm up to form a hand-off pocket. The halfback aims for the backside guard-center gap, and receives the ball. He reads the backside guard-center gap and runs to daylight (Diagram 4-8).

HALFBACK SCISSORS

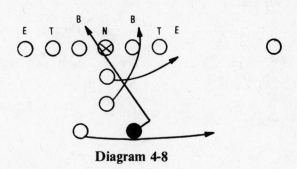

Diagram 4-8

Coaching Point: The trap blocking scheme is especially effective with this play.

The inside counter attack is only four plays but with four blocking schemes provides 16 looks to a defense. These 16 variations enable the Multi-Bone to attack a fast-flowing defense with tremendous flexibility.

THE OUTSIDE COUNTER ATTACK

The purpose of the outside counter attack is to threaten the entire width of the field on every play. This is the basic concept of the

Delaware Wing T. The outside counters threaten the defense's backside tackle, end and secondary.

The outside counters provide an additional style of running the ball and are another way of getting good halfbacks the ball.

Line Blocking for the Outside Counters

The line blocking for the outside counters is base blocking. The blocking schemes for this phase of the multi-bone attack are not interchangeable. Each counter has certain schemes that can be used with it. The outside options can use some triple option schemes and the counter power plays can use some power blocking schemes.

For any option the perimeter adjustments are the same as for the triple option. The "crack," "hook," "TED" and "load" calls add great flexibility to the counter attack.

Counter Slant

The Multi-Bone counter slant comes directly from the twin veer dive play. This play was taken from Lou Holtz's attack and adopted to the Multi-Bone. This play was also the basis of Bud Wilkinson's split T (Diagram 4-9).

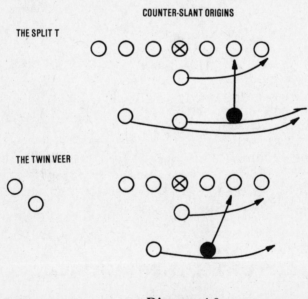

COUNTER-SLANT ORIGINS

THE SPLIT T

THE TWIN VEER

Diagram 4-9

The counter slant has a place in the Multi-Bone Attack because of the counter action of the play and the quickness of the dive. Giving the play a counter look has the following effects:

1) It makes fast-flowing linebackers very vulnerable.
2) It gives better blocking angles to the line.
3) It exploits pinching defensive tackles.
4) It provides another style of running the football.
5) It adds the best of the Twin Veer attack to the Multi-Bone.

The two blocking schemes used for the counter slant are the "on-trap" and "Base" scheme. Both are described in detail in Chapter 3. The tight end blocks as though it were the belly play.

BACKFIELD ACTION

The fullback and offside halfback jab step away from the slant and give a good head and shoulder fake away from it. After the fake, they pivot back toward the slant and sprint to the sidelines at top speed.

The quarterback reverse pivots as quickly as possible and hands off to the diving halfback. The quarterback's reverse pivot moves him back into the backfield which allows the hand-off to take place deep in the backfield. This gives the ball carrier running room. After the hand-off, the quarterback accelerates down the line of scrimmage.

The diving halfback aims for the inside leg of the offensive tackle. He keeps his inside arm up forming a large hand-off pocket. After getting the ball, he reads the block of the offensive tackle. The tackle is taking the defender any way he can. The play could break

THE COUNTER SLANT

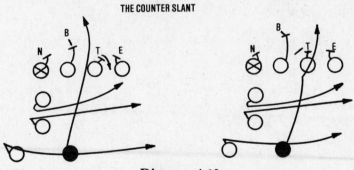

Diagram 4-10

inside against a looping tackle or outside against a pinching tackle. The halfback's shoulders should be parallel to the line of scrimmage. Positive yardage is the main objective (Diagram 4-10).

> **Coaching Point:** The halfback must have his eyes looking directly at the butt of the tackle. He cannot look for the handoff because the play is such a quick hitter.

The Counter Option

The counter option was also borrowed from Lou Holtz's Twin Veer attack. It is possible to attack the entire width of the field with this play when combined with the triple option. A defense cannot stop both the triple option and the counter option. The counter option is effective because it:

1) Attacks a backside defensive tackle pursuing flat down the line of scrimmage.
2) Attacks a backside defensive end who is closing down on the counter slant.
3) Attacks a secondary that is being depended on to stop the triple option.
4) Stops inside linebackers from getting into the perimeter.
5) Provides an alternate option attack.
6) Gives the linemen blocking angles on defensive personnel, enables them to handle a physcially superior line.
7) Provides another way for the halfbacks to get the ball.
8) Coordinates with the entire offensive package. The quarterback has the same pitch read as he does in the triple option.

LINE BLOCKING FOR THE COUNTER OPTION

In addition to the base blocking scheme, two other triple option schemes are used. These schemes are zone and "X" blocking both described in Chapter 3.

Base blocking for the counter option is taught as though the play were a sweep. The onside tackle must get outside position on the defender over him. The reverse crab block is used if the tackle is having difficulty.

> **Coaching Point:** The reverse crab block is taught as follows: 1) The tackle drives his outside shoulder to the inside breast of the

defender. This action should draw the defender down into the guard-tackle gap. 2) The tackle then whips his hips to the outside knee of the defender. This places the offensive tackle looking into the offensive backfield with his tail pointing toward the defense's goal line. He scrambles on all fours to maintan the block (Diagram 4-11).

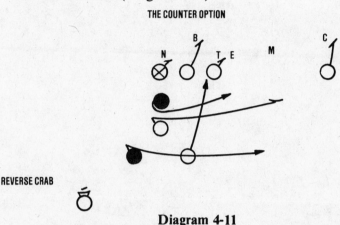

THE COUNTER OPTION

REVERSE CRAB

Diagram 4-11

TED blocking for the counter option differs from TED blocking for the triple option. The tight end combo blocks with the offensive tacke. If the tight end can see the side of the defensive tackle, he slams him before going after the linebacker. If the tight end cannot see the side of the tackle, he goes directly for the linebacker.

Zone blocking can be effective if 1) the defensive tackle is playing an inside shade, 2) the tackle is usually pinching, or 3) the play is run to the split end side. It is not used as often as the base scheme, but it is useful versus an exceptionally quick linebacker. The zone assignments are the same as in the triple option except that the diving halfback replaces the fullback on the double team with the guard (Diagram 4-12).

"X" blocking is used because it provides good angle blocks especially against an eagle or split four defense. This scheme is also effective against a defensive tackle who closes down with the offensive tackle (Diagram 4-13).

Hook or crack blocks add versatility to the perimeter. These are also described in Chapter 2 (Diagram 4-14). Otherwise the receivers execute their stalk block.

COUNTER OPTION—"ZONE" BLOCKING

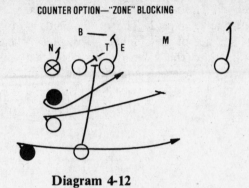

Diagram 4-12

COUNTER OPTION—"X" BLOCKING

Diagram 4-13

PERIMETER BLOCKS

"HOOK"

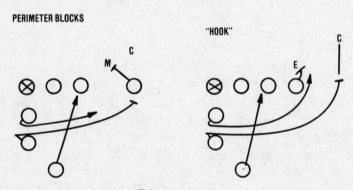

Diagram 4-14

BACKFIELD ACTION

The initial backfield paths are exactly the same as the counter slant except the quarterback fakes the ball to the diving halfback. The big difference between the counter option in the Twin Veer attack and the Multi-Bone counter option is that the Multi-Bone counter option can employ the fullback as a lead blocker while the Splitback Veer attack does not have that luxury. The Multi-Bone combines the benefits of the Splitback Veer attack and those of the full bone attack.

The dive back in the counter option aims for the inside leg of the offensive tackle and blocks the first defender he sees. This could be an inside backer in base blocking (Diagram 4-11), a double team with the guard in zone blocking (Diagram 4-12), or a closing defensive tackle in X blocking (Diagram 4-13). By diving to the proper aiming point and continuing on his path, the dive back will find a defender to block. Regardless of the blocking scheme, the dive back's block occurs in the guard-tackle gap.

The fullback is the only player in the counter option who must learn something new. He must block the man responsible for the pitch. That could be a rotating corner, a strong safety or an outside linebacker in a split four type of defense (Diagram 4-15). He must execute the same type of block he would use on the sweep. He cuts the outside knee of the second unblocked defender he comes to. In other words, the quarterback will option the first unblocked defender, and the fullback must block the second. This technique is not new to him; the only new aspect of the play is locating the pitch defender. But due to the counter action of the play this is not a problem. However, the fullback must be prepared for all possible situations.

The quarterback executes the play as he would the counter slant except he does not put the ball into the dive back's belly. Instead he flash fakes to him. As soon as he reverse pivots, the quarterback's eyes must go immediately to the defensive end. He must beware of the crashing defensive and be prepared to make an early pitch. The quarterback's reads of the defensive end are the same as in the triple option (see the Quarterback Play section of the triple option). The only new situations the quarterback must be aware of is a slanting defense in which the defensive tackle is going to play the quarterback. If the TED block is used, there is no problem. But if a zoning block is used, and the quarterback sees the tackle locked in with the defensive tackle, he must duck upfield inside the tackle's block (Diagram 4-16). With the X blocking scheme, if he sees the guard kicking out the defensive tackle, the quarterback ducks inside the guard's block and gets upfield for as much yardage as he can

FULLBACK BLOCKING FOR COUNTER OPTION

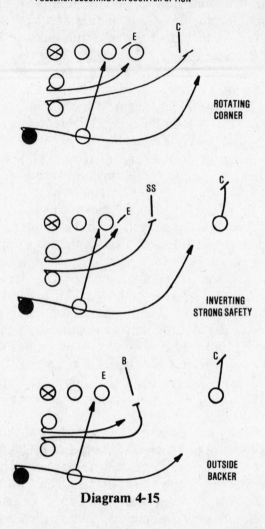

Diagram 4-15

(Diagram 4-16). This is a great play because the dive back also serves as a lead blocker. The read of the quarterback helps prevent the defense from rolling their secondary to one side and slanting to the other.

The pitch back again does exactly as he does in the counter slant except in the counter option he gets on the outside hip of the fullback and follows him just as he would follow the lead blocker in the triple option (see Triple Option Chapter).

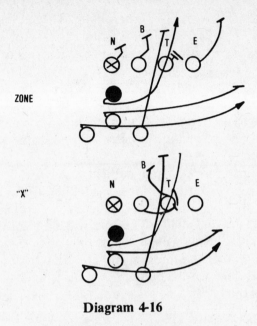

Diagram 4-16

OPPOSITE COUNTERS

The opposite counters are instant counters. They take little additional teaching in either backfield play or line blocking and produce five counters that can really destroy a defense's keys. The word "opposite" after option, belly, or sweep simply means that the fullback goes in the opposite direction of the play, and the quarterback reverse pivots in the opposite direction of the play. Another call, "halfbacks opposite," on a fullback dive or fullback counter produces a counter play inside to the fullback. These opposite counters, copied from the Delaware Wing T, add a lot to the attack with very little effort.

Option Opposite

The option opposite is a great misdirection option and is another way of getting to the perimeter. This option is especially effective against a split four look. The split four tries to defense the fullback with the inside linebackers. By the counter action, our lead back's block on the outside linebacker is also made easier. This option is also effective against any defense with a middle linebacker because he usually flows with the fullback.

The backfield action is very simple. The fullback dives in the opposite direction of the play and "dents" the line of scrimmage. The halfbacks execute their normal option routes just as they would in the triple option. The quarterback reverse pivots, flash fakes to the fullback and immediately gets his eyes on the defensive end. He must under no circumstances put the ball into the fullback's stomach and must always be prepared for a quick pitch. Once he reverse piviots he simply executes his read of the defensive end just as he would in any other option.

All perimeter blocking adjustments used in the triple option can be used here. These include load, crack, hook, and TED. The line blocking is always base; or "X" if there is a problem controlling a linebacker (Diagram 4-17). The line will be totally familiar with these blocking schemes already. This play also helps control inside backers and allows the linemen to get better angles on them. This play also produces a misdirection option from a broken bone set (Diagram 4-18).

OPTION OPPOSITE

Diagram 4-17

MISDIRECTION OPTION

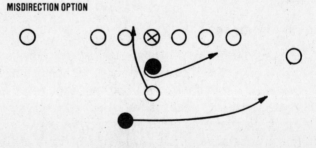

Diagram 4-18

Sweep Opposite

The sweep opposite has a remarkable resemblance to the buck sweep of the Delaware Wing T attack because that is where it originated. The only difference is that a pitch is used rather than the hand-off because a pitch takes less time to practice. The fullback action in the opposite direction makes the entire line blocking much easier. The linemen usually get good blocking angles on the linebackers. The linemen block this play with base blocking, and the backfield action is the same action as the sweep except the fullback is going in the opposite direction. A Wing-T type of sweep evolves from this one simple adjustment (Diagram 4-19).

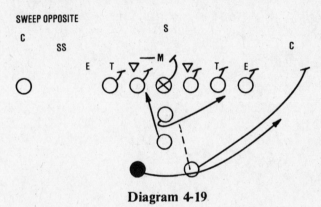

Diagram 4-19

Belly Opposite

The belly opposite also comes from the Wing T playbook. It is similar to the old split T cross-buck. The advantage of this play over the Wishbone is the lead blocker. This play can be used in several different situations:

1)   to make the block angles more effective;
2)   to provide another type of power misdirection;
3)   to provide another way to get the ball to the halfback;
4)   to take advantage of a team with one middle linebacker;
5)   to take advantage of any team keying our fullback.

Two blocking schemes, base and TED, are used with this play. In the base scheme, taking the defensive linemen any way they want to go eliminates the need to overpower anyone. With the TED

Scheme, which is used in some short yardage situations, the blocking angles are good for going off-tackle.

The backfield action is also very simple. The fullback dives opposite the direction of the play and must "dent" the line of scrimmage. The quarterback reverse pivots, flash fakes to the fullback and continues to execute his normal belly hand-off. The lead blocker reads the butt of the tackle and blocks accordingly (Diagram 4-20). The ball carrier follows the lead blocker, gets his shoulders parallel to the line of scrimmage and gets upfield for as much positive yardage as possible.

BELLY OPPOSITE

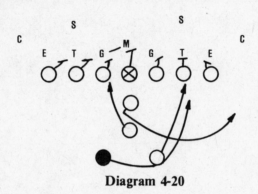

Diagram 4-20

Fullback Counter—Halfbacks Opposite

Some teams key the halfbacks and ignore the fullback. In this situation the fullback counter (see Diagram 4-5) can be effective with the halfbacks going in opposite directions and the quarterback reverse pivoting after his hand-off to the fullback and going in the opposite direction (Diagram 4-21). The line blocking schemes available are the same as with the fullback counter: base blocking, fold blocking, trap blocking, wedge blocking. The only teaching point is that the halfbacks go in the opposite direction of the play. This action is an excellent key breaker.

Veer Opposite

Veer Opposite has exactly the same backfield action as the option opposite. But veer blocking is used instead of base or TED blocking. The offside guard pulls and executes a "running reach" block on the first man outside the tackle's block.

FULLBACK COUNTER-HALFBACKS OPPOSITE

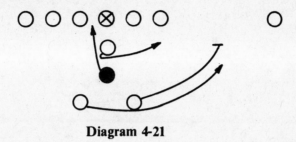

Diagram 4-21

This blocking scheme is used if the defensive tackle is closing down with the offensive tackle either in the triple option with veer blocking or in the trap blocking scheme.

The pulling guard uses the same technique he uses in the trap blocking scheme except that instead of going into the line of scrimmage he stays *on* it. He tries to get his inside shoulder on the outside hip of the first defender outside the tackle's block. He pins or seals him inside, isolating the defender whom the quarterback is optioning. The only drill needed for this blocking is to acquaint the pulling guard with the situations he will face: 1) a closing tackle; 2) a pinching tackle so he will pick up the scraping linebacker; or 3) a tackle who fires upfield whom he should just trap, knowing that the quarterback will duck inside his block (Diagram 4-22).

The backfield action and the quarterback reads are exactly the same as the option opposite. The fullback fills for the pulling guard and is responsible for the offside linebacker, or a lineman playing over the guard.

> **Coaching Point:** The quarterback should be aware of the possibility of a defensive tackle firing upfield. In that case, he will have to duck up inside the pulling guard's block.

The load block is yet another adjustment that can be used.

The entire misdirection attack is simple (only two new blocking schemes) and provides a counter for all of the backs in order to damage any set of defensive keys. The four inside counters with their four blocking schemes and the five outside counters with those multiple schemes provide 28 misdirection plays that can be run without repeating any. This strong misdirection game can produce an entire offense that can be used until the defense slows down its pursuit.

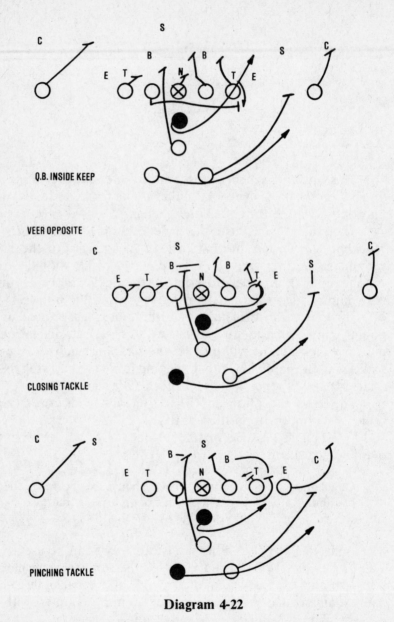

Diagram 4-22

CHAPTER 5

Drills for the Multi-Bone
Running Attack

Learning the technical aspects of the Multi-Bone running attack is just part of the process of putting this offense to work. Teaching the Multi-Bone to a team is another important phase of producing a winner. The drills designed to help teach the Multi-Bone running game were carefully selected. When taught properly and executed well, they will help to perfect the skills necessary for Multi-Bone offensive personnel.

In order to obtain the greatest benefits from the drills, the following guidelines are suggested:

1) Each drill must have a definite purpose.
2) Each drill must have some relation to the Multi-Bone offense.
3) Each drill must begin with the normal cadence.
4) Each drill should come as close as possible to actual game conditions.
5) Each drill should end with the whistle.
6) Any drill involving live tackling must have a quick whistle.
7) Each drill should have a recognizable name so no time will be wasted reviewing explanations more than once.
8) Each drill should be fast-paced and never drawn out to the point of boredom.
9) Have alternate drills available to help eliminate boredom.
10) The theory that repetition yields execution must be impressed upon the players throughout the day.

The Multi-Bone offensive drills are divided into three categories:

1) Line drills which are sub-divided into technique, take-off, and assignment drills.
2) Backfield drills which are sub-divided into blocking and ball-carrying drills.
3) Team drills in which the line and backfield work together.

LINE DRILLS FOR THE RUNNING GAME

The Blocking Progression

The first series of line drills is a blocking progression. This progression starts with the finished block and works backward to the beginning of the block. The drills should be done each day, but as the season progresses fewer repetitions will be necessary. These drills are specifically designed to help the linemen use proper form on their drive blocks.

Name of Drill:	THE FIT DRILL
Objectives:	To teach offensive linemen the position they should be in after contact is made. Also, to develop a wide base when driving the dummy.
Equipment:	Stand-up blocking dummies.
Starting Position:	Offensive linemen start this drill by actually laying their shoulders on the dummy. (They do not *hit* the dummy, but start with their shoulders on the dummy).
Procedure:	After getting into the proper "blocking fit," the offensive line drives the dummies until the whistle.
Coaching Points:	1) Linemen must have head up, neck bulled and flat back. 2) Linemen must alternate blocking shoulders. 3) Linemen must drive dummy with a wide base.

Diagram: 5-1.

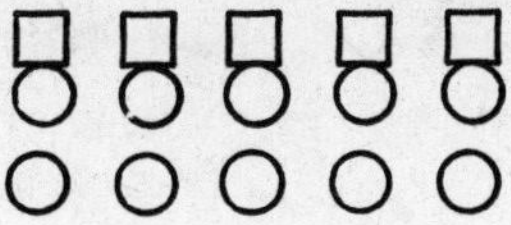

Name of Drill:	TWO-POINT AND FOUR-POINT SLED DRILL
Objectives:	To get the offensive line into the proper "fit." Also, to help take-off to the block.
Equipment:	Seven-man sled.
Starting Position:	A two-point stance, then a four-point stance.
Procedure:	From the two-point stance the line takes one step to their "blocking fit" and drives the sled until the whistle. Then from their four-point stance, they repeat the procedure.
Coaching Points:	1) The line should be looking directly at the coach while driving the sled. Head up.
	2) Wide base while driving.
	3) Use right shoulder first, then repeat with left shoulder.
	4) This drill can also be made into a leg drive drill by having a lineman behind each dummy standing on the sled to weigh it down.

Diagram: 5-2

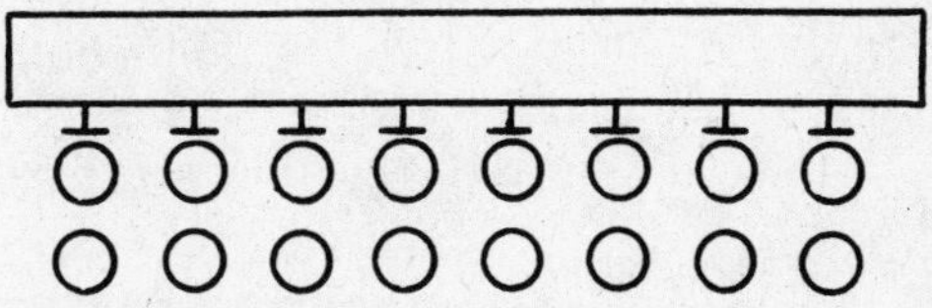

Name of Drill:	BOARD DRILL
Objective:	To drive with a wide base and a flat back.
Equipment:	Planks and blocking dummies.

Starting Position:	Four-point stance.
Procedure:	The dummies are placed on the end of the plank. The lineman fires out and drives the dummy the length of the plank. This drill is also done live.
Coaching Point:	The right shoulder is used first, then the left.

Diagram: 5-3

Name of Drill:	SHADES DRILL
Objective:	To teach line to execute a drive block when defender is on his outside shoulder or when he is on his inside shoulder.
Equipment:	Blocking dummies.
Procedure:	First, dummies are placed on inside shoulders of linemen and a drive block is executed. The same group of linemen have the dummies shading their outside shoulders. A reach block is then executed. This drill is also done live.
Coaching Point:	Linemen must execute both blocks with both right and left shoulders.

Diagrams: 5-4

5-5

The next two drills are designed to improve take-off. These drills are done daily and before the game.

Name of Drill:	BROAD JUMP
Objective:	To improve explosion from stance.
Equipment:	None
Starting Position:	Four-point stance.
Procedure:	Linemen execute standing broad jumps to cadence.
Coaching Point:	Linemen must stay low, striving for a horizontal explosion rather than a vertical one.

Diagram: 5-6

Name of Drill:	TAKE-OFF
Objective:	Emphasis of initial quickness off the ball.
Equipment:	None
Starting Position:	Four-point stance.
Procedure:	Line does a five-yard sprint
Coaching Point:	1) Must emphasize low body position. 2) Always check for good stance

Diagram: 5-7

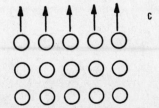

ADJUSTMENT DRILLS

The next series of drills is designed to practice the variety of blocking schemes or adjustments. These drills are all done in the following manner. The defenders hold shields. They are told what reaction to make by the line coach who stands in as the quarterback. The defenders slant (right or left) or play straight. The following schemes are practiced: 1) veer, 2) combo blocks, 3) "X", 4) zone, 5) fold, 6) trap, 7) on-trap, 8) base blocking, 9) veer-opposite, and 10) wedge blocking.

BACKFIELD DRILLS

The backfield drills are divided into blocking drills and ball-carrying drills. One of the key advantages of the Multi-Bone is that backs must be able to both block and run with the ball. This is not like the I Formation in which the fullback is a blocker and the tailback is a runner. There is no prima donna in the Multi-Bone backfield.

Backfield Blocking Drills

Having a lead blocker in the backfield is the key to the full bone. The lead blocker sets the Multi-Bone apart from the Splitback Veer attack. The importance of perfecting this lead block is obvious.

All backfield blocking for the running game uses the same technique so both fullbacks and halfbacks can participate in the same drills. This reduces practice time considerably.

The first phase of the blocking progression is done exactly as the linemen's progression. The backs first drill is the Fit Drill. They execute it the same as the linemen (see page 96). The next is the Two-Point Sled Drill (see page 97). There are three objectives to these drills: 1) to get the backs familiar with the position they should be in while making the block; 2) to develop the leg drive needed for the block; 3) to discourage a back from diving at a defender.

The next series of drills is designed for the backs.

Name of Drill:	SPRINT AND BLOCK DRILL
Objectives:	To execute the lead blocks from a stance. To teach backs to perform the blocks on moving targets. To

teach backs to sprint and still get
into the proper fit.

Equipment: Dummies and blocking shields.

Starting Position: Normal stances.

Procedure: There are two parts to this drill. In
the first part the backs line up in
their stances about five yards from
stand-up dummies. On the snap
count they sprint to the dummies
and execute their blocks. In the
second part the backs do exactly
the same thing except the dummies
are replaced with shields. These
provide moving targets. The
players holding the shields move
laterally away from the blocks.

Coaching Point: The coach in charge of the drill
always fakes a hand-off to the
fullback.

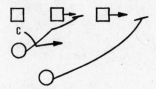

Diagram: 5-8

Name of Drill: FULLBACK DRILL

Objective: To teach the fullback whom to
block and to teach the path theory.

Equipment: One shield and one dummy.

Starting Position: Normal stance.

Procedure: Dummy (defensive tackle) and
shield (inside backer) are aligned
in a Fifty front. They either pinch
or sit and read. The fullback
blocks either the scraping backer
or the reading tackle.

Coaching Points: 1) The coach naturally fakes a
hand-off to the fullback.
2) The player with the shield

should make the fullback work by getting as much width as possible. 3) This drill can also be done by adding an offensive tackle.

Diagrams: 5-9

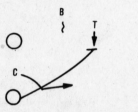

5-10

Name of Drill:	THE HALFBACK DRILL
Objective:	To teach the path theory for both the lead and the load block.
Equipment:	Two shields.
Starting Position:	Normal stance.
Procedure:	There are two parts to this drill. In part one two players with shields are placed five yards downfield and either invert or rotate. The lead blocker must pick out the defender responsible for the pitch and lead block him. Then the two players with shields are stacked on the line of scrimmage, and the halfback must repeat the procedure. In part two the players remain stacked on the line of scrimmage, but now the lead blocker picks out the player responsible for quarterback and load blocks him.
Coaching Points:	1) The backs must always stay on

their path regardless of the situation.

2) The players with the shield must make a good defensive reaction.

Diagram: 5-11

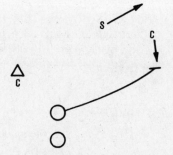

Name of Drill:	**RECEIVERS' STALK DRILL**
Objective:	To teach the stalk block against various defensive reactions.
Equipment:	Blocking shields.
Starting Position:	Normal stance.
Procedure:	A defender with a shield gives the receiver various reactions: 1) rotating, 2) dropping off, 3) freezing. The receiver executes the stalk block until the whistle.
Coaching Points:	1) The tight end must work on his release from the line of scrimmage. 2) This drill can progress to a live drill.

Diagram: 5-12

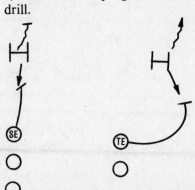

Ball-Carrying Drills

The next series of backfield drills is designed specifically to increase running ability. Although great runners have God-given talent, running drills will develop an average ball-carrier's ability. Most of the running drills are done in every offense: for example; running through tires, exploding through two dummies, one-on-one drills and the gauntlet drill are common to all offenses. The only drills discussed in this section are those unique to the Multi-Bone. These drills are done by all backs, including the quarterbacks.

Name of Drill:	THE SPEED DRILL
Objectives:	To teach the ball carrier to use the entire width of the field, and to teach the ability to turn the corner.
Equipment:	None.
Starting Position:	Normal stances.
Procedure:	Two backs face each other. The ball carrier on the three-yard line and the tackler on the goal line. The ball carrier can go when he is ready and outruns the defender to the flag.
Coaching Points:	1) The ball carrier should not use any moves, just speed. 2) He must dip his inside shoulder when turning upfield.

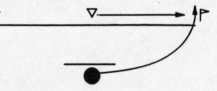

Diagram: 5-13	

Name of Drill	747 DRILL
Objectives:	To teach backs how to score. To create team spirit (this drill leads the league in fun). To give the backs a feel for scoring. To teach the vaulting-over-the-line technique.

Equipment:	Tackling dummies and old mats.
Starting Position:	Normal stance.
Procedure:	Five or six dummies are piled up on the goal line. Mats are placed in the end zone. The backs take off from their stances, take a hand-off and get airborne over the dummies.
Coaching Points:	1) Backs should run normal goal line plays like the halfback counter, belly or fullback dive. 2) Each back should have a shot at scoring. 3) This drill is a lot of fun for the backs.

Diagram: 5-14

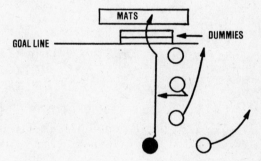

The Quarterback Progression

The quarterback progression begins with just the quarterbacks and proceeds to the entire backfield. The objective of the progression is to drill the quarterbacks on every detail involved in running the triple option. The basis of the Multi-Bone running game is the triple option and the quarterback is the key to the triple. These drills not only develop the physical mechanics of the triple option, but also develop the quarterback's confidence.

Name of Drill	FAST BREAK DRILL
Objectives:	To develop the quarterback's pitch technique and to develop the accuracy and strength of the pitch.
Starting Position:	Three quarterbacks five yards apart in two-point stances.

Equipment:	None.
Procedure:	The quarterbacks move at half speed the width of the field, pitching the ball back and forth. When they reach the far sideline, they turn around and come back.
Coaching Points:	1) Each quarterback should get a turn in the middle. 2) This drill should be done daily.

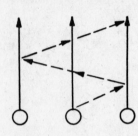

Diagram: 5-15

Name of Drill:	QUARTERBACK'S STEPS DRILL
Objective:	To teach quarterbacks the initial steps of the triple option.
Starting Position:	Three quarterbacks behind the centers spaced ten yards apart.
Equipment:	None.
Procedure:	One quarterback calls the cadence. The center snaps the ball and the quarterback takes the 45 degree angle step. Next a fullback is added to the drill. The quarterback takes his initial step, meshes with the fullback and rides him into the line. He either gives or keeps and sprints "downhill" to the next center. The quarterbacks rotate with each center.
Coaching Points:	1) This is a pre-season drill which is discontinued after the first two weeks of pre-season. 2) The quarterbacks must be comfortable with their steps

before progressing to the next drill.

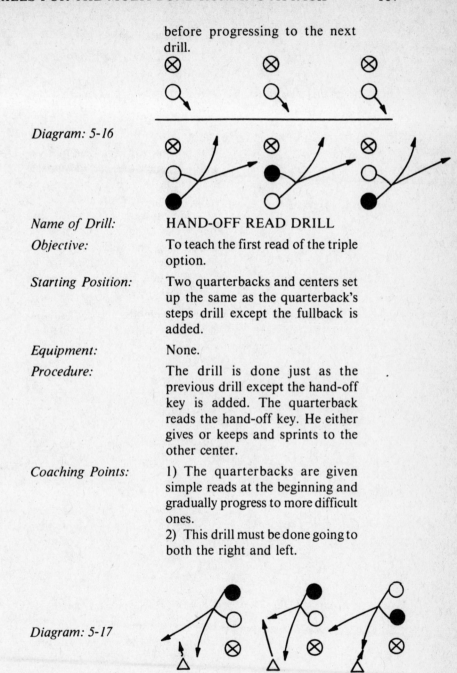

Diagram: 5-16

Name of Drill:	HAND-OFF READ DRILL
Objective:	To teach the first read of the triple option.
Starting Position:	Two quarterbacks and centers set up the same as the quarterback's steps drill except the fullback is added.
Equipment:	None.
Procedure:	The drill is done just as the previous drill except the hand-off key is added. The quarterback reads the hand-off key. He either gives or keeps and sprints to the other center.
Coaching Points:	1) The quarterbacks are given simple reads at the beginning and gradually progress to more difficult ones.
	2) This drill must be done going to both the right and left.

Diagram: 5-17

Name of Drill: THE TRIPLE DRILL

Objective: To teach and perfect all aspects of the triple option.

Starting Position: A center, a complete backfield and a receiver.

Equipment: Blocking shields.

Procedure: The second fullback becomes the hand-off key, the second quarterback plays the pitch key, a substitute halfback plays the pitch defender and the second split end plays the defender who has the deep third. The triple option is run against these "defenders" while the backfield coach signals the defense their assignments.

Coaching Points: 1) Each defender has a shield and delivers a blow on his assigned man.

2) The backfield coach gives the "defense" a variety of stunts to prepare the backfield for all situations.

3) Load and crack blocking adjustments are used.

Diagram: 5-18

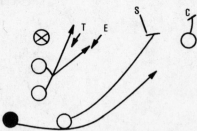

Name of Drill: HALF LINE READ DRILL

Objectives: To provide blocking coordination between line and fullback. To help the quarterback read the triple with various blocking schemes.

Starting Position; The setup of this drill is: a center, guard, tackle, quarterback and fullback against a group of defensive players using shields.

Equipment: Shields.

Procedure: They are aligned in a front by the line coach and execute one of a variety of stunts. The quarterback reads the defense with the fullback and either gives or keeps. The following fronts should be practiced against: Sixty, Split four, Fifty, Eagle, over-shifts and goal line defenses. Slants and pinches are practiced from all fronts. Veer, Zone and X blocking are used. The quarterback makes his hand-off reads.

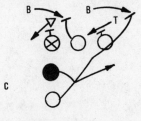

Diagram: 5-19

Name of Drill: VICTORY DRILL

Objectives: To build team precision. To develop team momentum, spirit and hustle. Helps total team take-off.

Starting Position: Normal alignment.

Equipment: Blocking dummies.

Procedure: The offense is on the goal line with a dummy over each lineman. They have ten plays to go to the far goal line or 100 yards. They use all base plays and drive the ball down the field. When they get to the other goal line the linemen switch: the first offensive line holds the dummies and the second line drives down the field again.

Coaching Points: 1) Stress break from the huddle and sprint to the line.
2) Stress team take-off.
3) Emphasize going until the whistle.
4) Show the importance of momentum and the importance of quickness getting in and out of the huddle to sustain a long drive.
5) Hustle is habit forming.

Diagram: 5-20

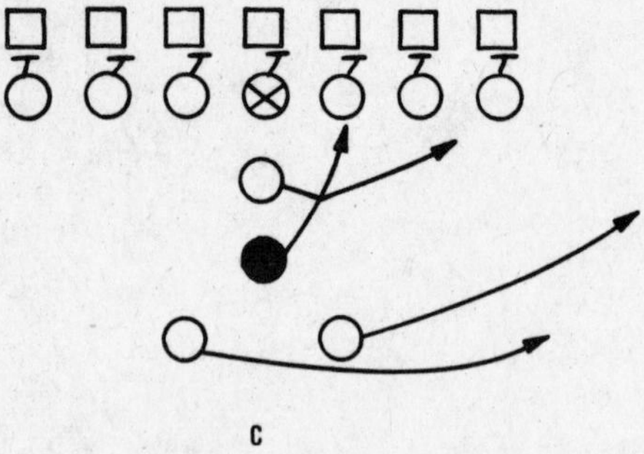

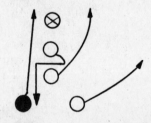

c

Name of Drill: PLAY CYCLES

Objective: To perfect the backfield action of the supplementary running game.

Starting Position: Normal alignment.

Equipment: None.

Procedure: Backfield runs all plays other than the triple option. These include the counter dive, belly, sweep, etc.

Coaching Point: Play cycles are done every day for nine minutes.

Diagram: 5-21

SCRIMMAGES

Both live and shield scrimmages are used throughout the season. Although this is not actually a drill, some points should be emphasized:

1) All live scrimmages are video taped. This may sound expensive, but if your school has a video tape machine, you can use the same tape over and over again.

2) We script every play so we know exactly who should be blocking whom. For example, we say, "Veer right against a Fifty pinch."

3) A different defensive reaction is shown on every play.

4) Every possible situation is scrimmaged during the course of the week. Normal downs, long yardage plays (third and eight, third and ten), short yardage plays (third and one), goal line offense and two minute offense are all practiced. This gives the offense a rehearsal for every possible stressful situation. When a team is accustomed to pressure, they react more efficiently when that situation arises in a game.

CHAPTER **6**

The Multi-Bone Play Action Passing Attack

One of the great advantages of the Multi-Bone attack is that because the multi-running attack is so simple and easy to install, it leaves 40 percent of practice time to devote to the passing attack. By devoting this amount of practice time to passing, a completely diversified passing game can be developed. One that can be both home-run or ball-control oriented.

Though the running attack can be devastating and has averaged as much as 6.0 yards per attempt over the course of a full season, passing must still be in the game plan. Passing must be considered a weapon and not a desperation move. Even when an offense seems unstoppable on the ground, it still must throw the ball. In the Multi-Bone Attack an effective passing game is an absolute requirement for the following reasons:

1) To move the ball on teams that are stopping the run.
2) It gives an offense "come from behind" capabilities. With it a team is never out of the game.
3) Teams over-committing to stop the run will be hurt by the pass.
4) Opponents do not have the practice time to prepare a sound defense for both the multiple running attack and the multiple passing attack.
5) Multiple sets confuse defenses and create errors in secondary coverages.

6) By *planning* to throw the ball, a passing situation does not create a feeling of panic.

7) By throwing the ball, the quarterback will develop confidence in the passing game.

8) The passing game can help control the ball and not just be a source of "home run" attempts.

9) The passing attack stretches a defense thus enhancing the running game.

OVERVIEW OF THE MULTI-BONE
PASSING ATTACK

The passing game from the Multi-Bone offense is more effective and efficient than passing from other styles of attack because the high-powered running attack causes adjustments and eliminations to be made by defenses:

1) It eliminates the popular five under, two- or three-deep secondary coverages which are the most difficult to throw against.

2) The secondary must be involved in run support. One member of the secondary must play either the pitch or the quarterback.

3) The split end is almost always single covered.

4) All the play passes are started off a running action because a member of the secondary will always have a run-support assignment.

5) The Multi-Bone passing attack and running attack are both executed from all the sets (see Chapter 1). This presents a recognition problem for the secondary.

6) Linebackers are rarely involved in underneath coverage because they must respect the run first.

7) Defensive backs cannot possibly get enough practice to become efficient at:
   a. defending the multiple passing attack;
   b. taking on the lead halfback's block;
   c. defending against the stalk block;
   d. recognizing the varied sets;
   e. recognizing the various perimeter blocking adjustments.

The key to passing effectively off this Multi-Bone offense is the integration of two completely different means of attacking possible opponents' reactions. These two means are united in the following ways:

1) By designing pass routes based on defensive reactions to the triple option and asking:
   a. Where do the free and strong safety line up?
   b. Who is playing the pitch?
   c. How good is the defensive back planing the split end?
2) Using possible patterns that can be run against a variety of defenses set up to stop the triple option (Diagram 6-1).

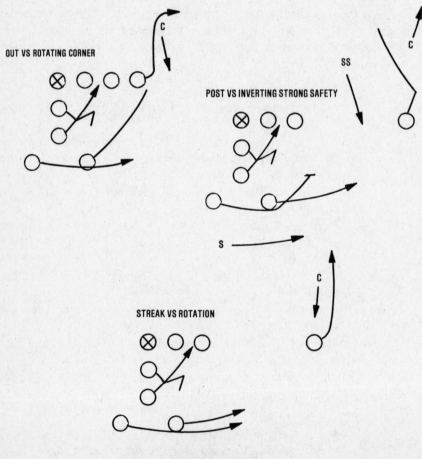

Diagram 6-1

    a. an out by the tight end against a rotating secondary;

    b. a post to the split end against an inverting strong safety;

    c. a streak to the split end against rotation to the split end.

3) Checking secondary adjustments to the multiple sets.

    a. Does the monster go to the strength of formation or to the wide side?

    b. What adjustment does the free safety make?

All the same sets that are used to run the ball are also used to throw the ball. Of course, the broken bone sets are advantageous in obvious passing situations.

The passing attack is kept simple for both the quarterback and the receivers. The needed flexibility in the passing game is accomplished by using three passing actions (play action, dropback, and sprint out). The receivers, however, learn one set of routes (Diagram 6-2).

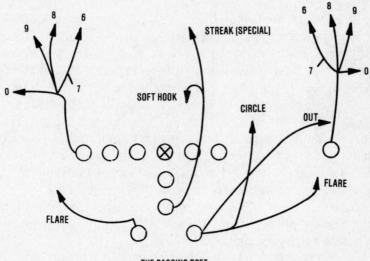

THE PASSING TREE

Diagram 6-2

The following routes are used in *all three* of the passing actions:

#0 (Out):	Seven steps downfield, then a 90 degree break to the sidelines.
#6 (Post):	Seven steps downfield (gaining width), then a 25 degree break to the post.

#7 (Curl):	Seven steps downfield, stop, turn in, and look for the ball.
#8 (Streak):	Six steps downfield, head fake an out, then break straight downfield without losing speed.
#9 (Flag):	Seven steps, head fake a post, then break on a 25 degree angle for the flag.

Coaching Points:
1) Receivers should always come off the line of scrimmage the same way regardless of the route.
2) Receivers should always gain width coming off the line of scrimmage by aiming a yard outside the defender.

THE PLAY ACTION PASS

Because the Multi-Bone is a run-oriented offense, the run action pass is an absolute necessity. The play action pass can exploit any weakness caused by an over reaction to the running game. The play action pass can also be a game breaker and "big" play producer. This alone is reason enough to make it a part of the offense.

Having a play action pass is important, but using it at the proper time is usually the cause for its success. A cardinal rule is that it must never be used in obvious passing situations. To use it on third and long defeats the entire purpose of the play. The dropback pass and sprint pass are used in obvious passing situations, and the play action pass is reserved for running situations such as first and ten, second and short, second and normal, etc. The play pass should have the element of surprise so that the defenders assigned to stop the run are still defending a run.

The play action pass can be thrown from all of the Multi-Bone sets, (see Chapter 1), but it is particularly advantageous to throw from the full bone sets because they are the most effective running sets. However, when the broken bone sets are being used very effectively as running sets, the play action pass becomes most effective from those sets.

The passes to be thrown stem from the basic running plays (Diagram 6-3). The more successful the running play, the greater chance the play pass has of working. If the defense has been forced to commit too many people to stopping the running game, then the

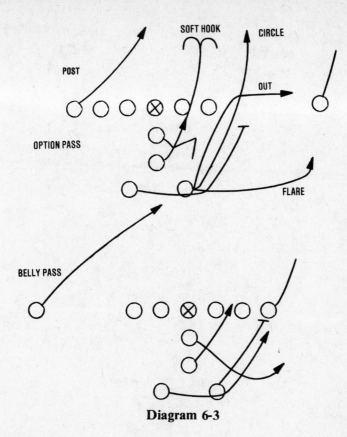

Diagram 6-3

play action pass will become more effective. To succeed it is important to ask two questions:

1) Why are the basic running plays either working or being stopped?

2) If they are being stopped by the secondary, what pass route will exploit this defense?

Note: If the defense is over-rotating they are vulnerable to the streak or the out. If the secondary is over-inverting, then the post route should be used (Diagram 6-4).

The routes used for the play action passing attack are exactly the same as those used in the sprint and drop-back actions (Diagram 6-2). The receivers need no additional learning. The "must" is to have the receivers approach the defenders as they would on a running play.

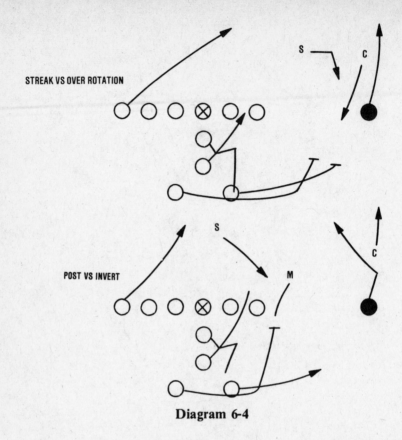

Diagram 6-4

The quarterback must have a good understanding of down and distance when using the play action pass. If it is second down (or third down in four down territory), the quarterback is instructed to throw the ball away if he's in doubt. But if it is the last down available to pick up the first down, the quarterback must run for the first down if his receivers are covered.

PASS BLOCKING

There are two pass blocking schemes that are used for the play action passing game: Normal and "Ice." Unless "Ice" is specifically called, the Normal scheme is used (Diagram 6-5).

Normal Play Action Pass Blocking

The play action pass blocking used the majority of the time is aggressive run blocking to the playside with seal and hinge blocking

PASS BLOCKING—"NORMAL"

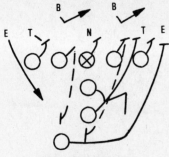

Diagram 6-5

to the blockside. The playside blocking is simple base blocking (Chapter 3).

The covered playside linemen fire their inside shoulders to the outside breastplates of the defensive linemen over them. They take the defender any way he wants to go.

The uncovered linemen check the backer that is over them. If the linebacker comes, an uncovered lineman blocks him, if the linebacker drops into his zone, he picks up the backside defensive end.

The fullback also reads the frontside backer. If the frontside backer scrapes, the fullback gets outside the tackle's block and picks him up. If the frontside backer blitzes, the fullback helps the guard. If the backer drops, the fullback releases downfield and does a soft hook (Diagram 6-6).

The offside halfback always blocks the first man outside the playside tackle's block.

The onside halfback runs either a flare or an out route. However, if the receiver on the line of scrimmage is doing an out, he does a circle route (Diagram 6-3).

Hinge Blocking

The center, backside guard and tackle use this technique. When hinge blocking, the lineman steps to the playside gap and seals. If no one comes, then he takes a 45 degree angle drop step with his outside foot and checks backside. If the lineman is uncovered and still not threatened, he drops deep to the "back door" to help on the defensive end.

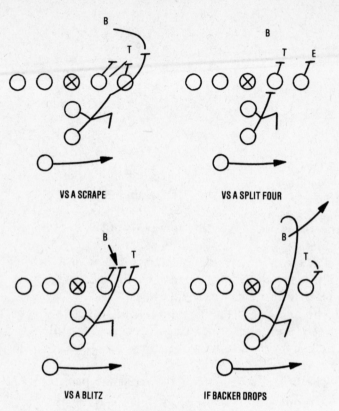

FULLBACK READS

VS A SCRAPE   VS A SPLIT FOUR

VS A BLITZ   IF BACKER DROPS

Diagram 6-6

Coaching Points:
1) If the backside lineman drops to pick up the defensive end, his path should be straight back at a 90 degree angle.
2) The center seals the backside gap against a split four defense, rather than the frontside.

"Ice" Blocking

This alternate scheme is very helpful against an active nose guard or against a split four.

The playside tackle blocks the first defender on the line of scrimmage from his inside gap to the outside. This would be the defensive tackle on him or the defensive tackle on the outside shoulder of the playside guard in a split four.

The rest of the line steps down and protects their backside gaps. If a lineman steps down and no one threatens his backside gap, he drops deep to pick up the backside defensive end.

The backfield follows the same rules as in their normal scheme. The fullback is responsible for the frontside linebacker and the offside halfback is responsible for the first defender outside the tackle's block (Diagram 6-7).

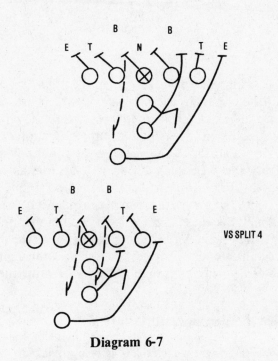

Diagram 6-7

Coaching Point: If the on-side halfback is needed to block, "Max" is called. Then he blocks the first defender outside the tackle's block and the offside halfback blocks the first defender outside the offside halfback's block (Diagram 6-8).

Option Dump Pass

Every triple option-based team must throw the dump pass. This is a quickie pass to either the split end or the tight end in the area of the secondary defender who has run responsibility.

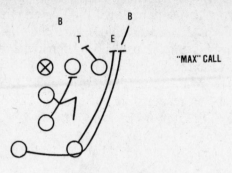

Diagram 6-8

The line blocking is either normal or "Ice" but the backfield action is different from the other play action passes. The onside halfback "load" blocks the defender responsible for the quarterback exactly as he does for the triple option (see Chapter 2). The offside halfback runs a sprint to the sidelines as though it were the triple option. Only the fullback's action is the same as the other play action passes. He is still responsible for the frontside linebacker.

The key to the play is the read of the quarterback. After his fake to the fullback his eyes go directly to the man responsible for the pitch. If he fires upfield, the quarterback dumps the ball to the end. But if the pitch defender hangs back for a pass, the quarterback runs, and looks for positive yardage. When in doubt, the quarterback runs.

> **Coaching Point:** By "load" blocking, the quarterback is given more time to make his decision because the defender responsible for the quarterback is being blocked.

The playside receivers release on a path that will take them directly to where the pitch defender is lined up. So, the tight end will run at the corner and the split end will usually follow the same path as when he executes his "crack" block. Once they release, they read the defender just as the quarterback does:

1) If the receiver sees the defender moving toward the line of scrimmage, he looks for the ball.

2) If the receiver sees the defender hanging, he checks the quarterback and makes sure he is not throwing. He then executes a block on the defender (Diagram 6-9).

OPTION DUMP PASS

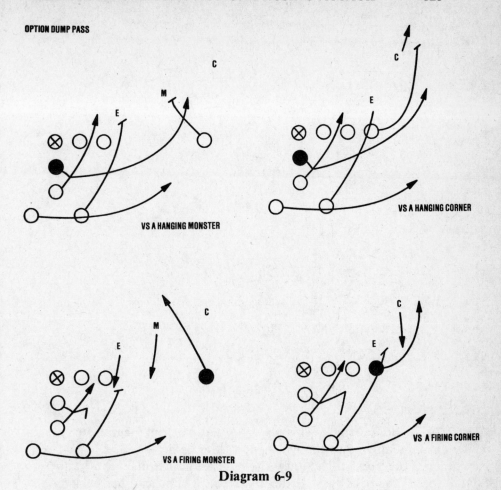

VS A HANGING MONSTER

VS A HANGING CORNER

VS A FIRING MONSTER

VS A FIRING CORNER

Diagram 6-9

Option "Opposite" Dump

This is executed exactly like the option dump pass, with one adjustment. The fullback goes in the opposite direction and the quarterback reverse pivots. This play can really be effective because the inside linebackers have a tendency to flow with the fullback (Diagram 6-10).

Option Bootleg

This play has been taken from the University of Delaware playbook. The bootleg of the Wing T is always troublesome to the defensive team accustomed to fast-flow option action. Option Bootleg is an attempt to accomplish the same effect within the

OPTION OPPOSITE DUMP

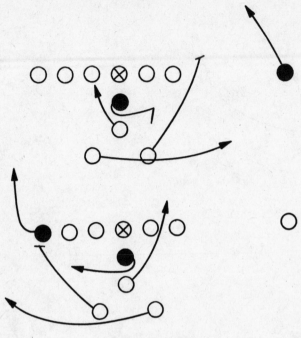

Diagram 6-10

Multi-Bone Attack. This play is run away from the monster who is usually aligned to the wide side of the field.

The backfield action is the same as the action for the dump pass for all the backs except the quarterback. The lead halfback "load" blocks, the trailing halfback sprints to the sidelines and the fullback fills for the pulling guard.

Coaching Points:

1) If the fullback fills for the guard and the line-backer drops off, the fullback releases on a curl route.

2) The trailing halfback can be used for a throwback pass if he has been left uncovered.

The quarterback fakes to the fullback, reverse pivots and sprints in the opposite direction of the action of the play. He must always look to break containment. The quarterback must also get a little depth, so he is moving upfield while he is reading the backside corner. If the corner comes toward the line of scrimmage, the quarterback sets up and throws to the tight end. If the corner comes toward the line of scrimmage but the tight end is covered by the safety, the quarterback throws to the split end in the deep middle. If the corner drops off to cover the tight end, the quarterback runs (Diagram 6-11).

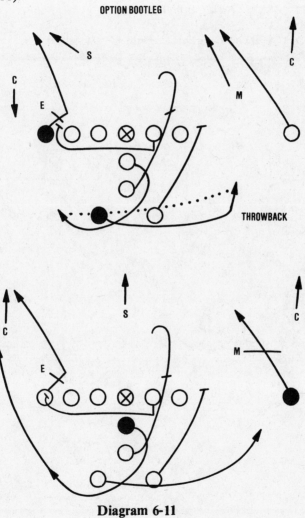

Diagram 6-11

The line blocks their normal play action pass blocking except for the guard in the initial direction of the play. The pulling guard pulls flat along the line of scrimmage and executes a "running reach block" on the first man outside the tackle's block. This is the same technique as used in veer opposite.

Coaching Point: The pulling guard must be prepared for four defender reactions:
1) A closing defensive end.
2) An end firing upfield.
3) A sitting end.
4) A dropping end (Diagram 6-12).

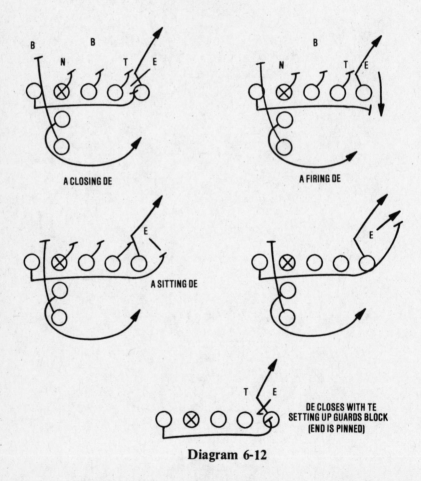

GUARDS BLOCKING

A CLOSING DE

A FIRING DE

A SITTING DE

DE CLOSES WITH TE
SETTING UP GUARDS BLOCK
(END IS PINNED)

Diagram 6-12

The receivers' routes are slightly different from the rest of the play action passing game. The tight end comes down on a defensive tackle and slams him with his inside shoulder. This will allow the offensive tackle to get better position on the defensive tackle. It will also cause the defensive end to close down with the tight end thus setting up the pulling guard's block (Diagram 6-12). After slamming the tackle, the tight end releases on a deep flag route. The split end sprints directly toward the deep middle zone (Diagram 6-11).

The option bootleg threatens the entire width of the football field in yet another manner. The bootleg also can be diversified further by throwing to the fullback, or by throwing back to the trailing halfback. Another variation can be run from the twin bone (Diagram 6-13).

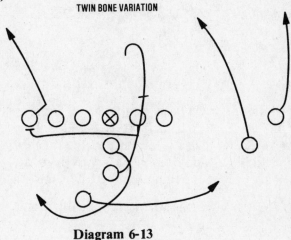

Diagram 6-13

SUMMARY

The play action pass can be devastating if a few simple rules are followed:

1) Use it in obvious run downs. Sometimes a high-percentage gamble can break a game open.
2) Try to take advantage of the pattern of run support from the secondary.
3) Never use it in an obvious passing situation.
4) Never rush the fake to the back.
5) Never force the ball to the receiver.
6) The line must be aggressive as in run blocking.
7) The quarterback must release the ball quickly, but intelligently.

CHAPTER **7**

The Multi-Bone Dropback
Passing Attack

An important phase of the Multi-Bone passing game is a simplified dropback attack. It is based on flare control of the linebackers, and a series of reads by the quarterback which allow him to throw high-percentage passes. A dropback passing attack is essential to the Multi-Bone for the following reasons:

1) It gives the offense an ideal weapon for long yardage situations.
2) It provides an effective two-minute offense.
3) It is a great complement to the triple option.
4) The backs can be released into passing lanes giving the quarterback five possible receivers.
5) It creates large seams in the secondary because the quarterback can use the entire field. (The sprint out limits the field because of the lateral movement of the passer.)

THE NUMBER SYSTEM

The patterns are called by using two numbers. The route of the widest receivers on the line of scrimmage is called by the first number. (i.e.: six is the post, seven is the curl, eight is the streak and nine is the flag). The second number indicates the direction of the fullback. Three is to the left and four is to the right. The second receiver to the side of the fullback's call does a route which will take him to the sidelines (Diagram 7-1).

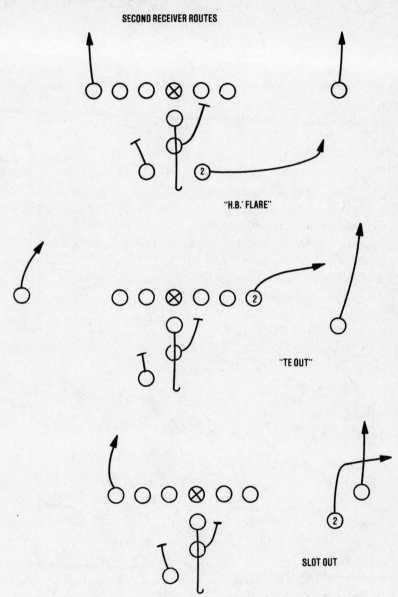

Diagram 7-1

Coaching Point: The second receiver could be:
1) A halfback who would do a flare route.
2) A tight end who would do an out
3) A slot who also would do an out.

Coaching Note: The tight end's out route in a Pro set is a modified out. Rather than take six steps downfield, he angles directly to the sidelines at a 45-degree angle (Diagram 7-1).

BACKFIELD PLAY

Once the backs know the direction of the play, their action is directly related to the play of the linebackers (Diagram 7-1A).

The fullback reads the first linebacker to his side. (This could be an inside linebacker in either a Pro or college four-three). If the linebacker is blitzing, he steps up to the line of scrimmage and blocks him. If the linebacker drops off, the fullback does a soft hook over the middle. Occasionally the fullback will run a streak. This is done with a special call (usually called "Fullback Special").

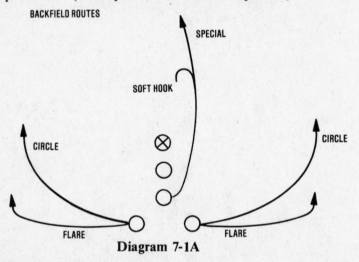

Diagram 7-1A

The offside halfback follows the same rules as the fullback while reading the linebacker to his side. The only difference is that the offside halfback does a flare instead of a soft hook if the backer drops.

The onside halfback always does a flare route unless "Max" is called, in which case he would execute his rules exactly as the offside halfback does. He would only release on a flare if the outside backer dropped off (see Pass Protection).

> **Coaching Point:** When the linebacker is blitzing, the back must come up to meet his charge. He should never sit back and wait. He must block the backer as close to the line of scrimmage as possible.

THE QUARTERBACK'S READS

An important part of the dropback game is the quarterback's reads. Multi-Bone quarterbacks are always reading keys, so this learning is a very simple procedure.

The first read for the quarterback is the free safety whom he should locate as he gets under the center. His first read is even before the ball is snapped. He divides the field into two halves (Diagram 7-2). He knows it is a balanced secondary when there are

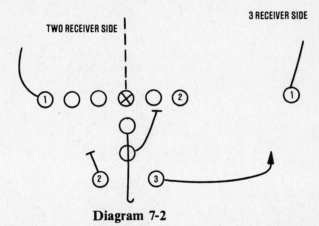

Diagram 7-2

two defensive backs on either side. If it is a balanced secondary, he will throw to the side where the fullback is going (Diagram 7-3). If it is an unbalanced secondary, (the free safety in the same half as the strong safety) he will throw to the two-receiver side because those receivers will be single-covered (Diagram 7-4). So he is throwing away to the half of the field where there is no free safety.

> **Coaching Point:** The quarterback can lure the free safety to a side by looking in that direction.

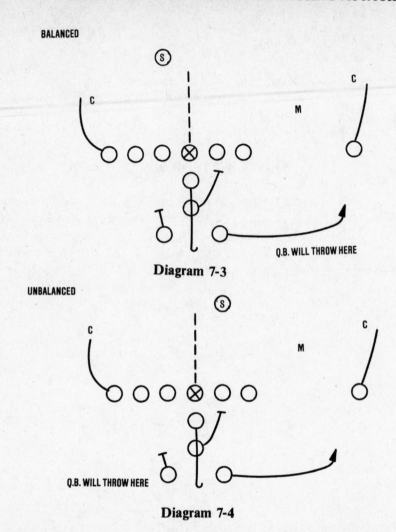

Diagram 7-3

Diagram 7-4

Our quarterback is also taught what secondary looks he may expect. The first and most popular is a "monster" to the wide side of the field with a three-deep secondary behind him. If facing this secondary coverage, locating the free safety is very simple. For example, if a "64" was called, the quarterback would be throwing to his right. However, if the FS was cheating to the wide side, he would throw to his left (Diagram 7-5).

The quarterback's next read comes after the snap of the ball. Now as he receives the ball, he immediately looks to the direction side linebacker. If the linebacker is blitzing, the quarterback knows

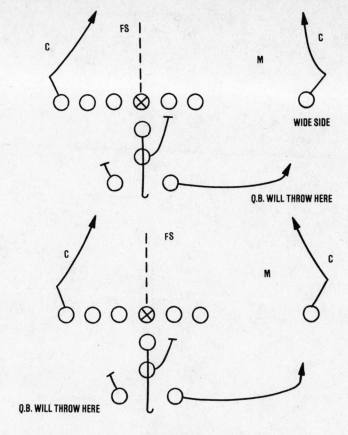

Diagram 7-5

that the receivers there are single-covered and will throw to the widest receiver. If the linebacker drops into the passing lane of the wide receiver, the quarterback will dump the ball off to either the flaring halfback on the two-receiver side or the fullback on the other side. (Diagram 7-6). If the quarterback finds everyone covered, he sprints to the butt of the center and executes a quarterback draw (Diagram 7-7).

Coaching Point: The quarterback's drop is always five steps.

Note: The quarterback has three options. He can pass to one of the widest receivers on the line of scrimmage, dump the ball to a running back, or run the ball on a quarterback draw. To

Q.B. LINEBACKER READS

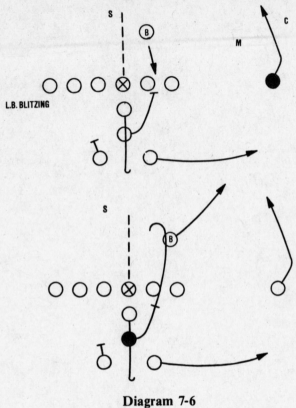

L.B. BLITZING

Diagram 7-6

Q.B. DRAW

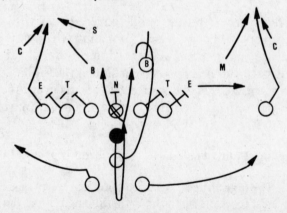

Diagram 7-7

determine which, is a very simple reading process since before the ball is snapped he knows to which side of the field he will be throwing and by his second step back he knows if the linebacker is coming or going. This read tells him which receiver he is going to throw to and if the receivers are covered, he runs. This amounts to a "triple option" passing game.

One of the nice things about dropping back from the Multi-Bone is that the patterns can be called away from the monster which always makes him wrong. For example, if it is established (via either scouting report or from the press box) that the monster is aligning to the wide side of the field, the pass is called to the short side (Diagram 7-8). This will force the defense to play a more balanced secondary which will also help the triple option become more effective.

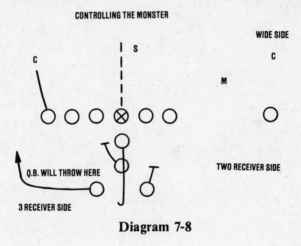

Diagram 7-8

The secondary, as stated earlier, cannot defend both the triple option and the dropback pass.

This fact leads to a simple "check with me" system. The quarterback calls "check with me" in the huddle. Once he comes to the line of scrimmage he reads the secondary and either calls: 1) the triple option if the monster is off the line of scrimmage; or 2) the dropback pass away from the monster if he is tight on the line of scrimmage (Diagram 7-9). This is a great first down call.

Note: This is a very unique integration of the running and passing games. A good pass defense cannot defend the triple option and a good defense against the triple option is ineffective

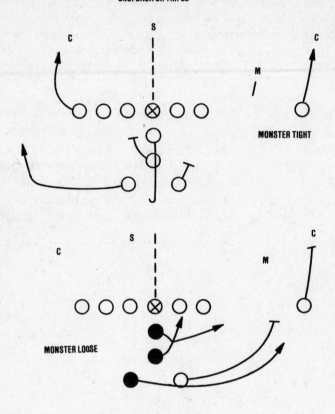

Diagram 7-9

against the dropback pass. (This concept was borrowed from Homer Rice.) Further control of the monster can be accomplished by using all the Multi-Bone sets described in Chapter 1.

DROPBACK PASS PROTECTION

The protection for the passer is very important and a good deal of practice time must be devoted to it. There are two basic dropback schemes: the normal scheme and the solid scheme. Unless "solid" is called, the normal scheme is used.

The normal scheme's rules are as follows:

Center: Any defender on or over. Against a split four, he blocks in the opposite direction of the fullback.

Guards:	The first down lineman on his side of the line of scrimmage. He checks his outside gap first.
Tackles:	The second down lineman on his side of the line of scrimmage. He checks his outside gap first.
Fullback:	Linebacker to playside (see backfield action).
Offside Halfback:	Linebacker to his side (Diagram 7-10).

"Solid" blocking is the alternate blocking scheme which is used in specific situations:

1) If a defense is constantly blitzing their linebackers.
2) If our center cannot block the nose guard.
3) If additional blocking is needed because:
    a. Our tackles cannot block the defensive tackles
    b. The quarterback is definitely throwing a deep pass.

The blocking rules for the "solid" scheme are:

Center:	The same rules as the normal scheme.
Guards:	The first defender to their side of the center either on or off the line of scrimmage. If they are uncovered and the linebacker drops off, the guard helps the center on the nose guard.
Tackles;	The second defender on or off the line of scrimmage to his side of the center. If the tackle is uncovered (as in a College 4-3) and the linebacker doesn't come, he helps the back on the defensive end.
Fullback:	Blocks the first defender outside the tackle's block to his side. If the defensive end drops off, he helps the tackle.
Halfback:	Follows the same rules as the fullback to his side (Diagram 7-10).

Note: Against a six-one both normal blocking and the "solid" call lead to the same blocking scheme.

Neither scheme is effective against an eight-man front without an adjustment. The first adjustment is the "Max" call which has been explained earlier. The second adjustment is the "hot" receiver principle.

The second receiver to the side of the play call (the fullback's direction) becomes the "hot receiver." If "Max" isn't called, the

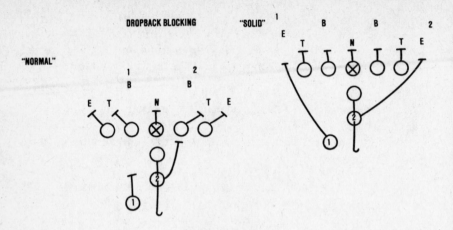

Diagram 7-10

"hot"receiver principle is used. When the quarterback comes to the line of scrimmage and sees an eight-man front, he knows the outside backer will be his first read. If the outside backer comes, he dumps the ball to the hot receiver. If the outside backer drops off, the quarterback proceeds with his normal reads (Diagram 7-11).

Dropback Blocking Technique

The dropback protection technique should be practiced daily because it is totally unique, and different from the rest of the attack. The dropback pass blocking technique is broken down into a series of coaching points and axioms.

    1) His initial step should find the blocker's outside foot splitting the assigned defender. Pop the defender under the chin with his outside shoulder and recoil.

Note: This will take the defender's initial charge away.

    2) Move feet as quickly as possible, always maintaining the inside position gained in Step 1.

    3) Keep as much separation as possible between yourself and the defender.

Note: If the defender to be blocked is a linebacker, set up a little deeper.

CONTROLLING AN EIGHT MAN FRONT

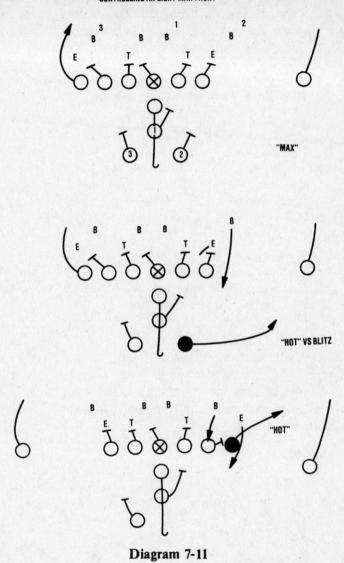

Diagram 7-11

4) Always keep elbows pointing to the ground; don't give the defender a handle to grab by keeping arms up.

5) Always know where the quarterback is ... point your "camera" at him.

6) Always be alert for cross-charges.

There are two key *coaching points* about the actual contact. First the lineman should be taught to fire *up* into defenders with a lunging action. Then second, once the blockers make the hit, they recoil, making sure to keep an inside position on the defender.

> **Coaching Point:** Dropback pass blocking is completely unlike the rest of the offense and must get specific attention each day.

THE QUICK DRAW

Another phase of the dropback game is the Quick Draw. This is a better play than the normal draw play because it provides the option of a pop pass, and no extra practice time is needed to teach backfield execution. The Quick Draw can be used to pick up a vital first down. It is easily adaptable to all the Multi-Bone sets, and can be used in any situation. For this play, the quarterback has two options: he either can throw a pop pass to the tight end or he can execute a quarterback draw, depending on the reaction of the linebacker to the side of the tight end.

As the quarterback takes the snap from center, he immediately looks for the linebacker to the tight end side. If the linebacker is blitzing he will immediately throw a pop pass to the tight end. If the linebacker is dropping into the passing lane, the quarterback will take two more steps backward and then sprint directly over the playside guard and read the tight end's block on the linebacker (Diagram 7-12).

QUICK DRAW

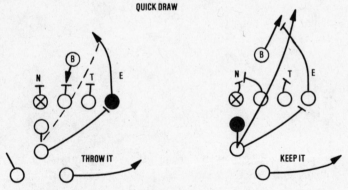

Diagram 7-12

Coaching Point: The tight end releases from the line of scrimmage and immediately looks for the linebacker to his side. If he sees him dropping back, the tight end blocks him. If he does not see the linebacker, he should immediately look for and expect the ball to be thrown to him. The tight end will know immediately whether he is a blocker or receiver.

The blocking scheme for this play is "solid," which was described earlier.

The Quick Draw does not produce game-breaking plays, but it is a completely safe play to produce a needed first down since it effectively controls linebacker drops. No matter what the linebacker does, he is wrong!!

SUMMARY

The dropback attack provides good capability to come from behind or succeed in long yardage situations. It also provides the weapons for changing the offensive style from a team that throws four times in one game to a team that throws 25 times in the next game without resorting to a "desperation" type of passing attack. The dropback game is based on quarterback options similar to the Multi-Bone running attack. It provides the needed explosiveness and a quick-score capacity to an attack that might be considered conservative. Finally, the dropback pass used in conjunction with the triple option presents an opponent's secondary with too many weapons to defend.

CHAPTER 8

The Multi-Bone Sprint
Passing Attack

One of the basic philosophies behind the Multi-Bone offense is that there must be more than one way of doing everything, no matter what phase of the attack. The passing game not only requires a play action series and a dropback attack, but also a sprint out attack.

The sprint out game is a very simple addition to the Multi-Bone scheme because the receiver's routes are exactly the same as in all other actions. No additional learning is involved. The blocking is the same as in the Multi-Bone running game so there is little to be learned in that area. The Multi-Bone quarterback should be a natural sprint out passer because of his required running ability, and there are no new reads to teach him or more importantly for him to absorb.

> *Note:* The sprint out will eliminate much of the stunting a defense can do since the quarterback is moving away from the blitzing pressure. Also, by having different launch points for the quarterback, a defense cannot "zero in on him." (This hinders their pass rush.)

The sprint out also gives the defensive end another thing to worry about, and it takes instant advantage of a "crashing" defensive end or a "feathering" end, two of the most common defensive techniques used against the triple option.

The last plus of the sprint out is that it provides an excellent goal line passing attack.

Note: Even pro teams are going to sprint out on the goal line.

The passing routes are exactly the same as those used in the dropback attack and are numbered in the same manner. Combo patterns are possible by calling two numbers. The first number is always the widest receiver to the playside. For example, "Sprint Right 70" means the widest receiver does a curl and the second receiver does an out. The offside end drags unless his route is specifically called (Diagram 8-1).

Special routes for the backside receivers can also be called. For example: "Sprint Right 707" means the backside receiver curls and becomes the prime receiver (Diagram 8-1).

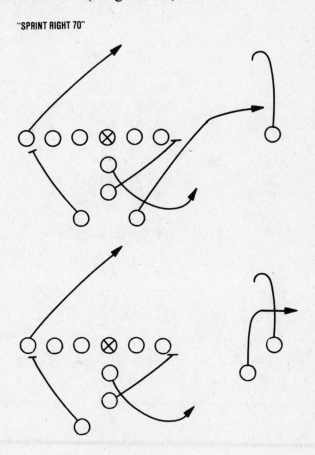

"SPRINT RIGHT 70"

Diagram 8-1

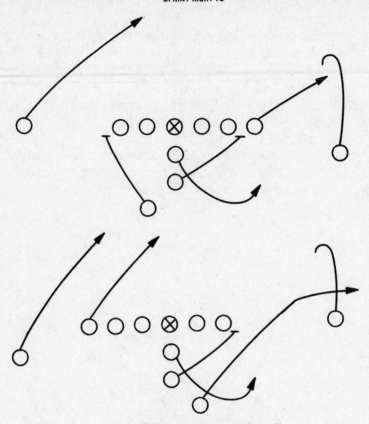

Diagram 8-1 (continued)

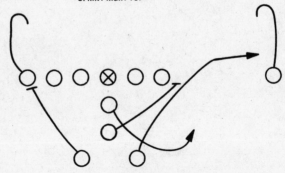

SPRINT RIGHT 707

Diagram 8-2

Coaching Point: When the call goes to a backside receiver, the quarterback must pull up behind the offensive tackle.

In the Multi-Bone sprint, two basic backfield flows are used. In the "Load" call, the onside halfback and fullback block exactly as they would on a sweep (see Chapter 3). The fullback blocks the first defender outside the tackle's block. The halfback either blocks the first defender outside the fullback's block, or if no one shows, he helps the fullback (Diagram 8-3).

ONSIDE BACKFIELD BLOCKING "LOAD"

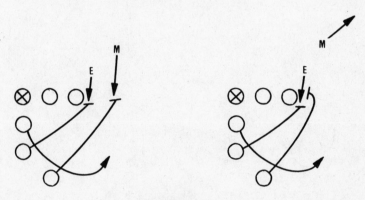

Diagram 8-3

Note: At times, the onside halfback is released on a pass route from this action (Diagram 8-1).

The "flare" call is exactly the same as the "load" call except the onside halfback does a "flare" route (Diagram 8-4).

ONSIDE BACKFIELD BLOCKING "FLARE"

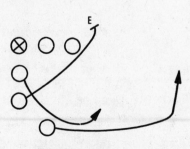

Diagram 8-4

The offside halfback always blocks the first defender outside the offside tackle's block, unless "back flare" is called, in which case he would do a flare route. For exmple, "Sprint Right 707 Back Flare" would look like Diagram 8-5.

The number of possibilities is really endless and can be varied from game-to-game with very little effort.

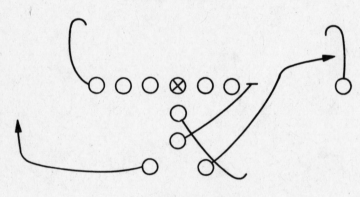

"SPRINT RIGHT 707 BACK FLARE"

Diagram 8-5

SPRINT OUT PASS PROTECTION

The frontside blocking is aggressive blocking, and is the same zone blocking used on the triple option (Chapter 2). Blocking rules are simple; handle all defensive fronts and stunts (Diagram 8-6):

Center:	First man from onside gap to backside gap. If no one, then check backer. No one, backside.
Onside Guard:	First man on the line of scrimmage from inside gap to outside gap. If no one then check backer; if no one, then backside.
Onside Tackle:	Same as onside guard.
Offside Line:	Step to protect inside gap. If no one, then check backside.

"X" blocking is used at times for variation and is executed as described in Chapter 2 (Diagram 8-7).

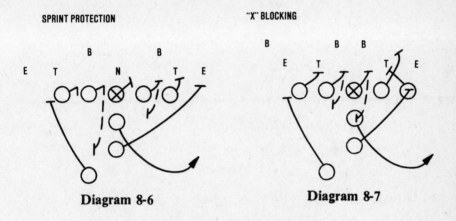

SPRINT PROTECTION

"X" BLOCKING

Diagram 8-6

Diagram 8-7

QUARTERBACK PLAY

The most important person in the sprint out attack is the quarterback. He is the one who makes it happen. It is imperative that he understands the concept behind the sprint out attack and his role in it.

He must know how many yards are needed for the first down. This makes his pass or run decision easier. As he takes the ball from the center, he must explode to get outside. He must not even consider throwing the ball until he is outside the offensive tackle.

Once he gets to the corner, he must think of throwing first or running if his receivers are covered. It is easier for him to assume the pass will be open, and react if it is covered, than plan to run and then have to throw if he is being rushed. So, as he gets to the corner he looks to his prime receiver. If the prime receiver is covered and the second receiver is in the quarterback's line of vision, he checks the second receiver. If the second receiver is covered, the quarterback runs. If the quarterback cannot spot the second receiver immediately, he runs. *When in doubt run.* For example, when running an "80" (Diagram 8-8), as he gets outside, the quarterback sees the split end covered but sees the slot open, so he fires to the slot. Two points to be stressed here: 1) never force the ball to a receiver, and 2) when in doubt, run. It is a good idea to practice this for nine minutes each day.

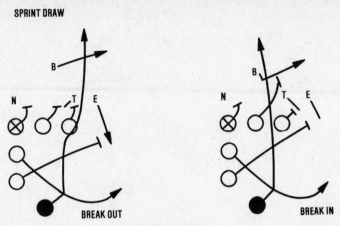

Diagram 8-8

Quarterback Technique and Learning Points

Quarterback technique in the sprint pass is extremely important, and the coach must be constantly aware of the following:

1) The quarterback's first step must be an open 45 degree angle step away from the center.

2. He must pull the ball to his heart immediately, holding the ball with two hands (similar to the "position" in the triple option).

3. The quarterback must explode from the center, gaining some depth as he goes.

4) His eyes must immediately go to the defensive end to read if he will be able to break containment (is the end crashing down or firing upfield?)

5) Always keep the ball in a throwing position.

6) Get outside and read the prime receiver.

7) When he is sprinting away from his throwing hand, the quarterback should turn his upper body and flip his hips to get ready to throw.

8) Break containment as soon as possible to pressure the secondary.

9) When in doubt, run.

THE SPRINT DRAW

The sprint draw is a running play, but it works well with the

Multi-Bone sprint out passing game. This play has been made popular by the "I" teams but is actually a better play from the Multi-Bone because of the alignment of the backs.

There are no steps to teach the Multi-Bone halfback because by alignment he is in position to receive the hand-off. There is also very little added teaching involved with the line and the fullback since they block their normal sprint out rules and the ball-carrying halfback runs to daylight. The following explains why the sprint draw is an effective phase of the Multi-Bone passing attack:

1) It takes advantage of a firing defensive end.
2) It can be run from all of the multiple sets.
3) It is a great way to get the ball to a gifted runner.
4) It exploits a defensive front that is shifted to the tight end side.
5) It takes advantage of a defense that tries to contain with the inside linebacker.
6) It is an all-weather play.

Line Blocking for the Sprint Draw

The line has nothing new to learn on this play. The blocking is normal zone blocking which is used in the running game. Occasionally "X" blocking is used, which is also used for the running attack (Chapter 2).

Backfield Steps

The fullback and offside halfback have nothing new to learn. They do exactly what they would do in the regular sprint out pass. The fullback blocks the first defender outside the onside tackle's block and the offside halfback blocks the first defender outside the offside tackle's block.

The onside halfback or ball carrier takes one lateral step in the direction of the play, then stops, makes a pocket for the hand-off (inside arm *up*), and waits for the ball. Once he gets the ball, he reads the guard-tackle gap just as he would a counter slant (Chapter 4). The play could break inside or outside (Diagram 8-9).

The quarterback explodes from the center exactly as he does on the sprint pass, but instead of looking to the defensive end, he looks to the halfback. He then places the ball in the halfback's hand-off pocket and continues on his sprint path.

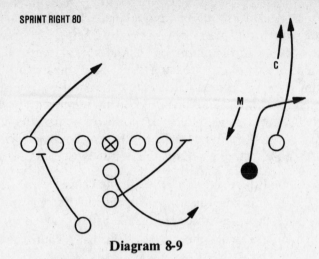

SPRINT RIGHT 80

Diagram 8-9

THE SPRINT DRAW PASS

The sprint draw pass is part of the sprint package and is easily incorporated into the Multi-Bone. The sprint draw pass call affects only two people: the quarterback who fakes the hand-off to the onside halfback, and the onside halfback who fakes a sprint draw. The line, receivers, and remainder of the backfield execute as though the word "draw" was never said. They follow their normal sprint rules (Diagram 8-10). This play can be run from any of the Multi-Bone formations.

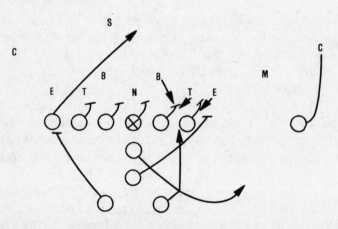

SPRINT DRAW PASS

Diagram 8-10

SUMMARY

The combination of the dropback, play action and sprint pass from the Multi-Bone, provides an explosive passing offense. In obvious passing situations there are two completely different manners of attack (drop back and sprint) with a minimal amount of learning. Also, the sprint pass and sprint draw combination will often account for quite a bit of rushing yardage, and this provides the passing attack with a hidden running dimension. Opponents have the unenviable task of trying to prepare for the running power of the Multi-Bone and three totally flexible passing actions.

CHAPTER 9

Drills for the Multi-Bone Passing Game

Teaching the Multi-Bone passing game is accomplished with exactly the same drill technique used to teach the running game. The drills break down the passing attack into stages and phases and emphasize each phase accordingly. Starting with the individual skills, and building to total team skills, is an age-old teaching device that has proved to be very effective.

The Multi-Bone passing drills are broken down into the following categories:

1) Line drills which are sub-divided into technique drills and assignment drills.
2.) Receiver drills which are sub-divided into catching technique running routes, and team drills.
3) Quarterback drills which are sub-divided into throwing and arm strengthening for the quarterbacks, reading drills and team drills.
4) Backfield drills which are sub-divided into catching, receiving, blocking, and team drills.

All drills are executed with the same guidelines as the running game drills.

LINE DRILLS FOR THE PASSING GAME

When drilling the offensive line for the passing game, no time is spent on take-off because that has already been taught. The only drills for the line are designed to teach the new techniques, unique to the passing game, that the lineman will have to execute.

Name of Drill:	SEAL AND HINGE DRILL
Objective:	To teach backside pass protection
Equipment:	Shields
Starting Position:	Normal alignment
Procedure:	ON the snap of the ball, the lineman take their seal and hinge steps while "defensive linemen" rush the passer. The "defensive linemen" are arranged in various defensive fronts.
Coaching Points:	1) This drill is done with shields or live, on occasion 2) Cross charges are practiced also.

Diagram: 9-1

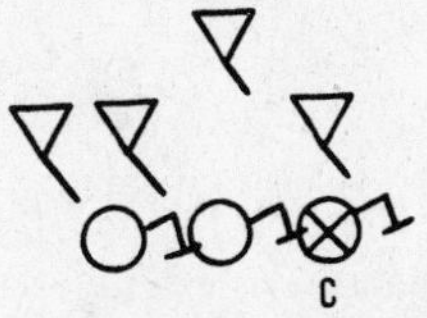

Name of Drill:	ONE-ON-ONE PASS BLOCKING DRILL
Objective:	To develop one-on-one pass blocking for the dropback passing game.
Equipment:	Shields
Starting Position:	Normal alignment
Procedure:	A defensive man is aligned over a lineman, and the defensive man is instructed to beat the lineman any way he can. A coach stands seven yards deep and if the defensive man can touch the coach within five seconds the defensive man wins.

Coaching Points:

1) The main difficulty in coaching the dropback pass block is the tendency for the linemen to lunge at the defender. The coach must be sure that the line's thrust is *up* into the defender not *out* at the defender.

2) This can be developed into a 15-point game between the offensive and defensive lines and can be a great spirit-building drill. The winning team is usually exempt from a couple of sprints.

3) On days with no hitting, this drill can be done with shields.

Diagram 9-2

Name of Drill: 5-ON-5 DROPBACK PASS DRILL

Objective: To block the pass rush

Equipment: Shields

Starting Position: Normal alignment

Procedure: The line is set up against the three popular defenses, and they block while the defenses use various cross-charges.

Coaching Points:

1) The linemen must wait for defenders to come to them and not chase them.

2) Normal and solid blocking used

3) Backs and backers are added to the drill during the season.

Diagrams: 9-3,

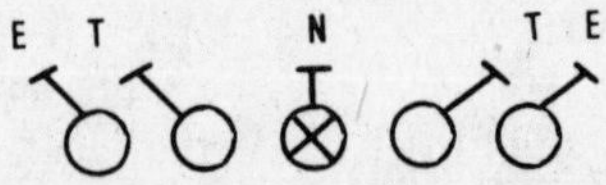

9-4

9-5   E   T   T   E

BACKFIELD BLOCKING DRILLS

Pass blocking for backs is an uncommon technique that must be practiced daily.

Name of Drill:	BLOCKING THE BACKER
Objective:	To teach the backs how to block the backers
Equipment:	Shields
Starting Position:	Normal alignment
Procedure:	The backs are set up with three backers to "read" and either block or release depending on the backers' reactions Shields are used for the backers.
Coaching Points:	1) The backs should meet the blitzing backer as close to the line of scrimmage as possible.
	2) The backs should block the backers above the waist. They should not dive at the backers' feet because the linebackers will step over them and destroy the quarterback.
	3) The backs are also set up with two defensive ends and the backs step up and block them or release if they drop off. This is what the backs do in the solid scheme.

Diagram: 9-6

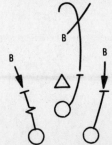

Name of Drill:	**FULLBACK SPRINT BLOCKING**
Objective:	To teach sprint blocking
Equipment:	Light dummy
Starting Position:	Normal alignment
Procedure:	The fullback aligns in his normal spot and is taught to block the first man outside the tackle's block, which is the technique he uses for veer blocking (see Drills for the Multi-Bone Running Game). The defensive end holds a light dummy and fires upfield, sits and reads, or closes down. The fullback attacks his outside knee.
Coaching Points:	1) The fullback makes his block alone, even though he will usually have a halfback to help him in a game situation. 2) The fullback violently attacks the outside knee of the defensive end and that is why it is wise to use a dummy instead of a player.

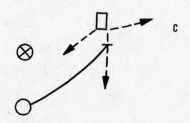

Diagram: 9-7

Name of Drill:	**DOUBLE SPRINT BLOCK**
Objective:	To teach the halfbacks to "clean-up" after the fullback
Equipment:	Light dummy
Starting Position:	Normal alignment

| Procedure: | Set up exactly as the previous drill with the defender using a light dummy and either firing upfield or closing down. However, both the fullback and halfback block the defender. |

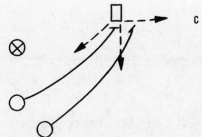

Diagram: 9-8

Name of Drill:	**OFFSIDE PLAY ACTION HALFBACK BLOCK**
Objective:	To get the offside halfback to sprint to the defensive end and block him on a play action pass
Equipment:	Light dummy
Starting Position:	Normal alignment
Procedure:	The defensive end, holding the lightweight dummy, gives the halfback three reactions; he drops off, fires upfield, or crashes.

Diagram: 9-9

DRILLS FOR THE RECEIVERS

In this book, many of the ideas about teaching the passing game have been borrowed from Homer Smith and have been adapted to the Multi-Bone. The basic theory behind drilling receivers for the Multi-Bone is this: the more the receiver practices catching the ball, the better he will become.

Stationary Catching

The receivers begin this drill the moment they step on the field for practice. They pair off and have a catch. They should look the ball into their hands and concentrate on catching the ball in front of their bodies with just their hands. The receivers should also practice completing each catch by tucking the ball away to be able to run with it. The following catches are performed:

1) One-Hand Stationary Catch—This is the same as above except the receiver catches the ball with either his right or left hand.

2) Over-the-Head Stationary Catch—The receiver turns his back to the passer and catches the lobbed pass either over his left shoulder or his right shoulder.

3) Over-the-Shoulder Stationary One-Handed Catch—This drill is the same as the previous drill except the receiver catches the ball with either his right or left hand.

Coaching Point: In all stationary drills, the receivers should be conscious of their hand position. Their thumbs should be together on passes higher than the heart or over the shoulder.

Moving Drills

Every coach has a series of receiving drills. The Multi-Bone Attack's drills are self-explanatory:

1   One-hand catch and go
2)   Bad-ball drill
3)   Moving-over-the-shoulder drill
4)   Curl and bump

THROWING DRILLS

The absence of a quarterback who can throw a rope is a poor excuse for an ineffective passing game. With proper practice and drilling, a quarterback's arm can be strengthened considerably. The following drills are done prior to the start of regular practice:

1) Seated throw.
2) Kneeling tosses.
3) Standing throw—object is to help the quarterback get used to using his hips to generate power in his throw.
    a. no-step throw
    b. wrong-foot-forward throw

Name of Drill:	QUARTERBACK PROGRESSION
Objective:	To teach quick setup and explosion from center
Equipment:	None
Starting Position:	Normal stances
Procedure:	Part I—Snap and Setup: T quarterback takes the snap from center, drops back and sets up. This is a quickness drill. The faster he sets up, the more time he has to throw.
	Part II—Snap and Sprint: The same setup as the previous drill except that the quarterback receives the snap from center and goes on his sprint route to the next center.
Name of Drill:	QUARTERBACK READ DRILLS
Objective:	To practice quarterback reads of defenders for dump pass, option bootleg, quick draw, option opposite dump
Equipment:	None
Starting Position:	Normal stance
Procedure:	The quarterback executes the following plays reading the defenders (Diagrams 9-13):
	1) Option Dump Pass (9-10).
	2) Option Opposite Dump (9-11).
	3) Quick Draw (9-12).
	4) Option Bootleg Read (9-13).

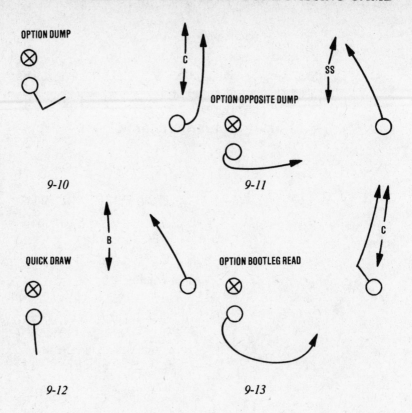

9-10   9-11

9-12   9-13

SKELETON PASS SCRIMMAGE

It is advantageous to have at least 18 minutes of skeleton pass scrimmage per day. The defensive backs, defensive linebackers, and defensive ends are involved. The defensive unit plays normal pass defense, and the offense runs the dropback or sprint passing attack. At least 12 minutes should be spent on the dropback and the remainder on the sprint out. The play action pass is never practiced in this drill because this is an obvious pass situation and the play action pass must never be used in an obvious passing situation. The quarterback reads the alignment of the free safety and the drop of the linebackers just as he would in the dropback attack. He has three seconds to throw the ball (Diagram 9-14).

SKELETON PASS SCRIMMAGE

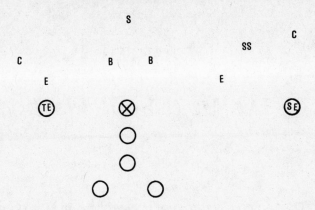

LIVE SCRIMMAGE

During the live scrimmage period, at least half the total number of plays called are passes. As with the running game, every play is script.

CHAPTER **10**

The Multi-Bone Playbook

This chapter is the complete Multi-Bone Playbook. The basic running and passing plays are diagrammed against six common defenses. The adjustments to each play have been explained in previous chapters.

The following points should be referred to when using this playbook.

Coaching Points:

1) Each play can be run to the right or the left.
2) All sets also can be called to the right or left.
3) In a broken bone set, the second receiver on the formation side becomes the lead blocker on all options in that direction.
4) All perimeter adjustments can be used with all option plays.
5) Each play has been explained in detail in previous chapters.

Multi-Bone Sets (Figure 10-1)

BASIC SET

WIDE

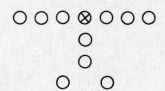

TIGHT

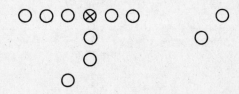

TWIN BONE

FLEX TWIN

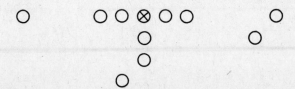

Figure 10-1 (continued)

HEAVY TWIN

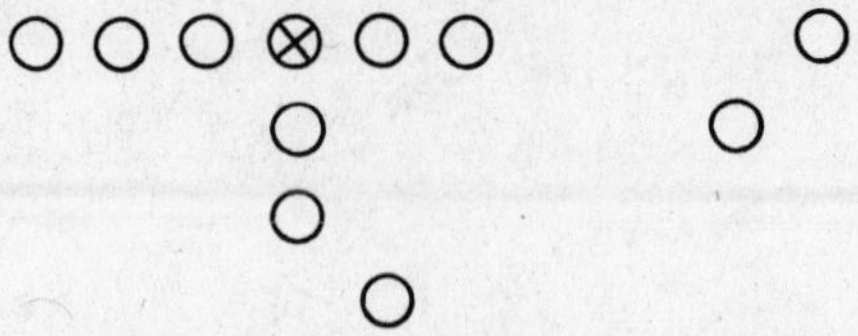

FLEX HEAVY TWIN

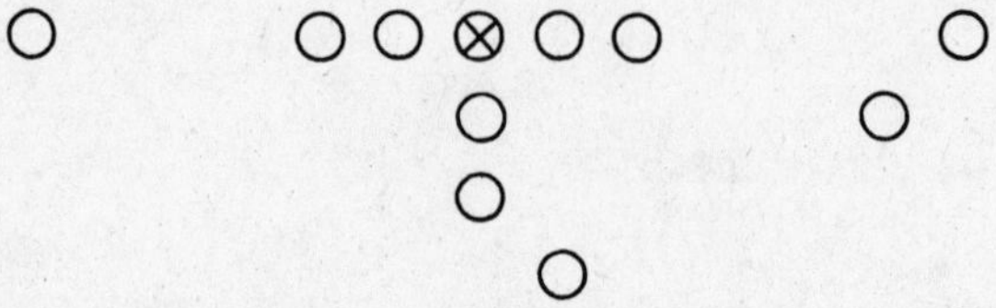

Multi-Bone Sets (Figure 10-2)
See Chapter 1 for explanations.

PRO BONE

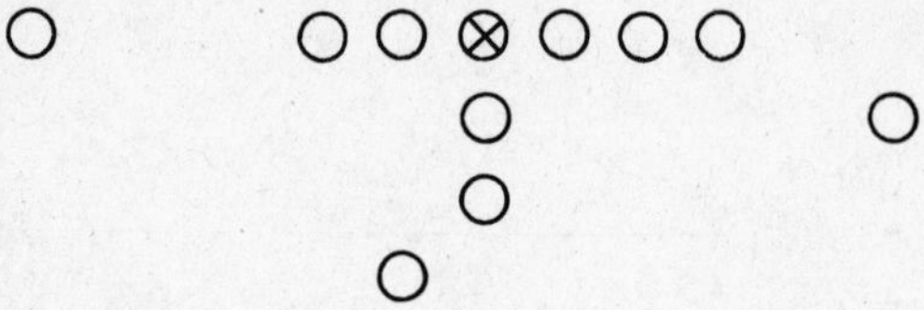

HEAVY PRO BONE

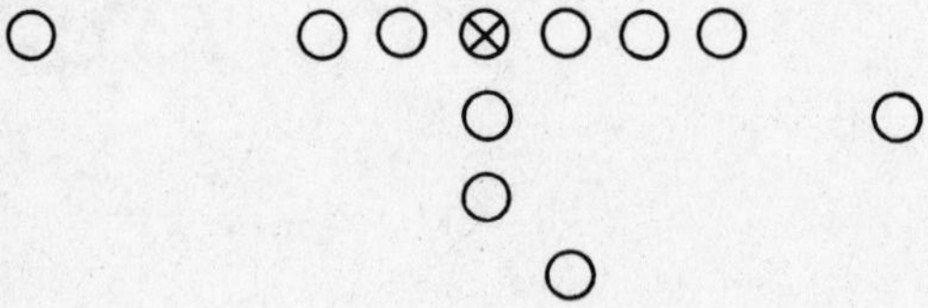

FLEX PRO BONE

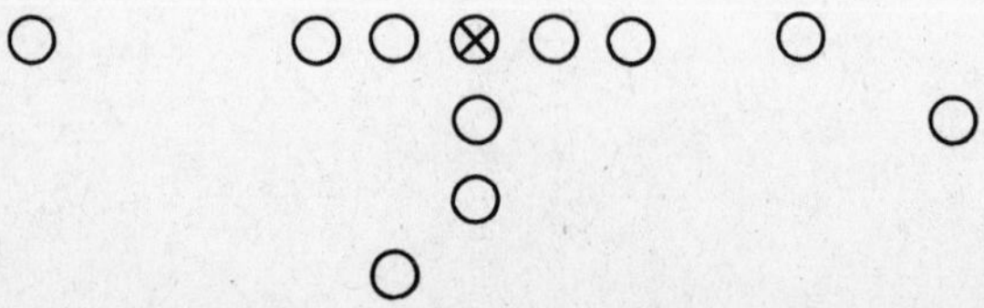

Triple Option—Veer (Figure 10-3)
See Chapter 2 for rules, assignments and coaching points.

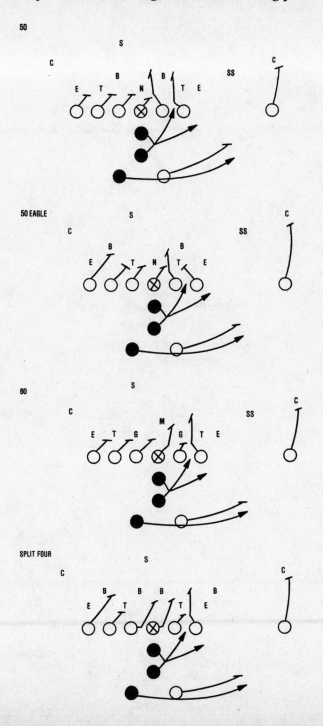

Figure 10-3 (continued)

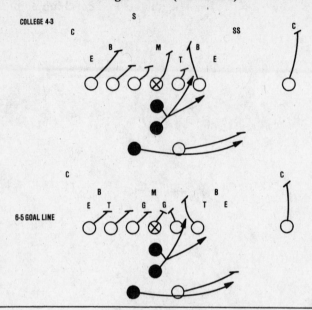

COLLEGE 4-3

6-5 GOAL LINE

Triple Blocking Adjustments
(Figure 10-4)

See Chapter 2 for rules, assignments and coaching points.

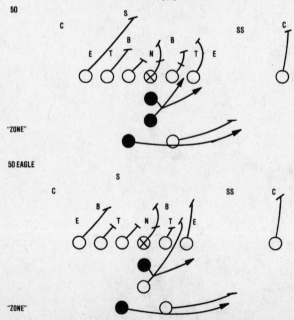

50

"ZONE"

50 EAGLE

"ZONE"

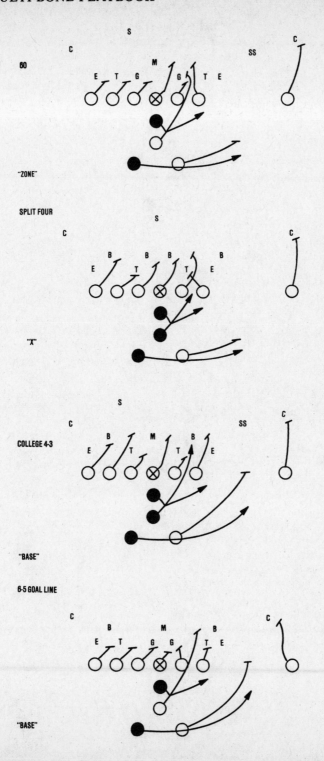

60

"ZONE"

SPLIT FOUR

"X"

COLLEGE 4-3

"BASE"

6-5 GOAL LINE

"BASE"

The Belly Play (Figure 10-5)
See Chapter 3 for rules and assignments.

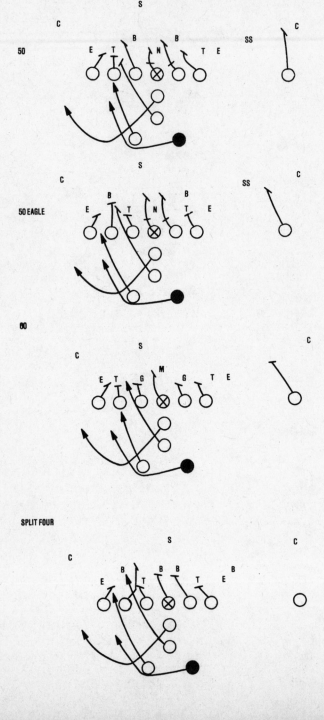

COLLEGE 4-3

6-5 GOAL LINE

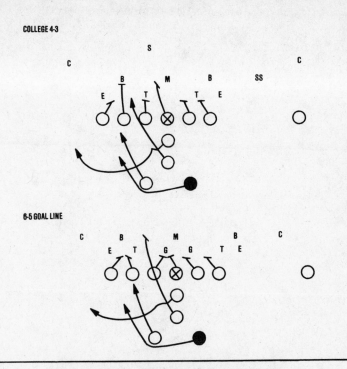

Common Belly Adjustments (Figure 10-6)
See Chapter 3 for rules and assignments.

50

"ZONE" IN PRO BONE

50 EAGLE

"ON-TRAP" IN HEAVY TWINS

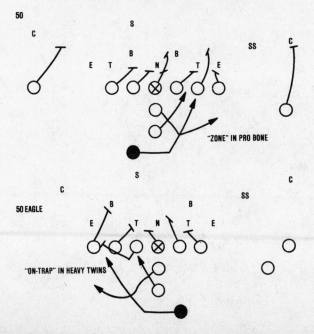

Figure 10-6 (continued)

60

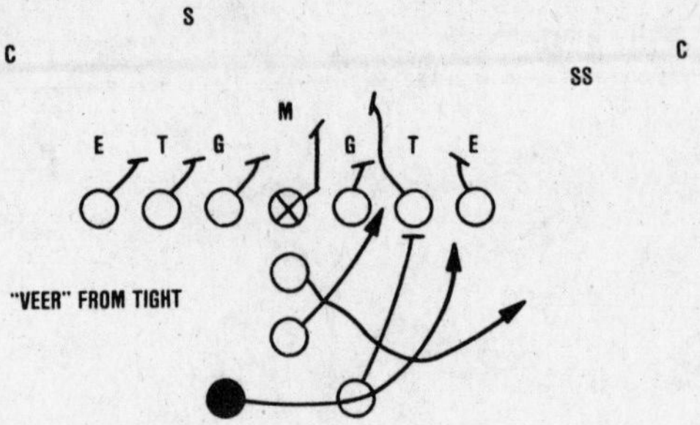

"VEER" FROM TIGHT

SPLIT FOUR

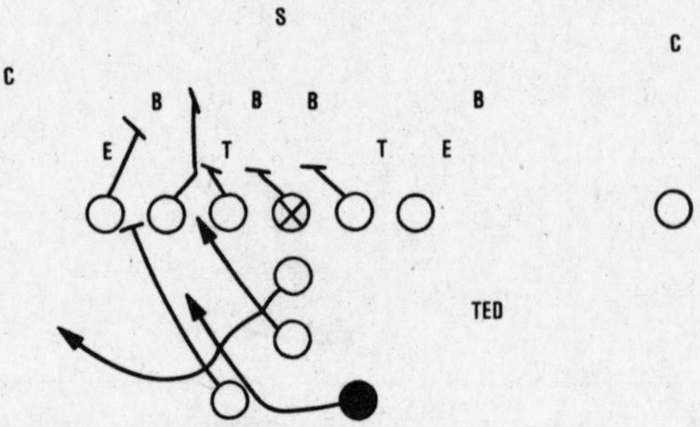

COLLEGE 4-3

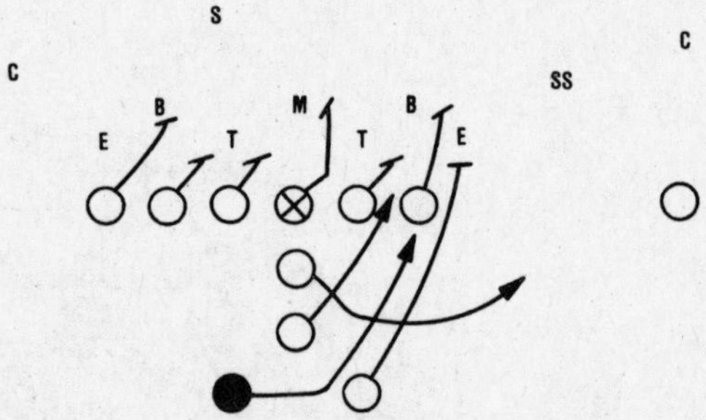

6-5 GOAL LINE

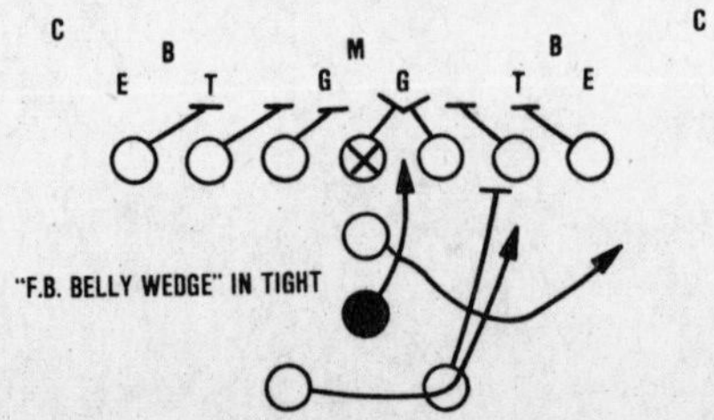

"F.B. BELLY WEDGE" IN TIGHT

The Fullback Dive (Figure 10-7)
See Chapter 3 for rules and assignments.

Figure 10-7 (continued)

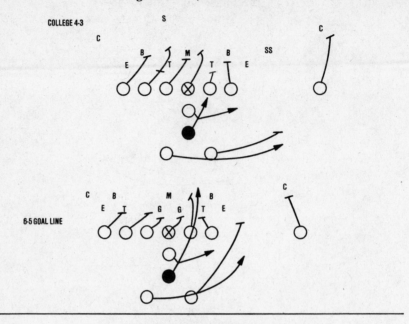

COLLEGE 4-3

6-5 GOAL LINE

Sweep (Figure 10-8)
See Chapter 3 for rules and assignments.

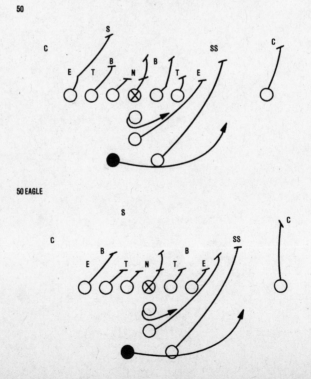

50

50 EAGLE

60

S

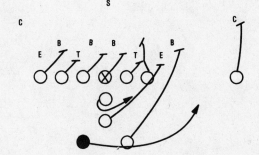

SPLIT FOUR

COLLEGE 4-3

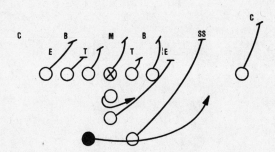

6-5 GOAL LINE

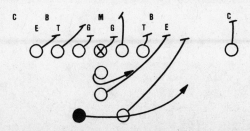

Fullback Counter (Figure 10-9)
See Chapter 4 for rules and assignments.

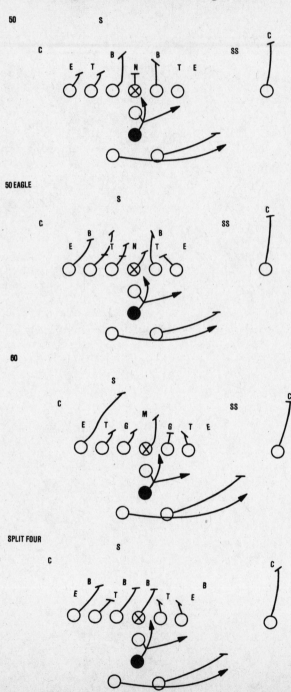

COLLEGE 4-3

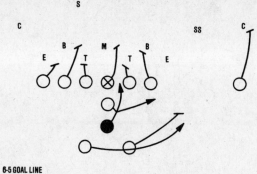

6-5 GOAL LINE

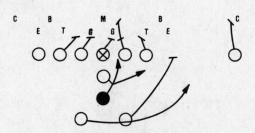

Halfback Counter (Figure 10-10)
See Chapter 4 for rules and assignments.

50

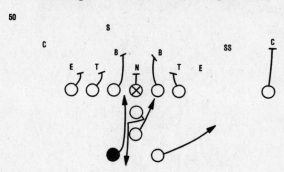

50 EAGLE

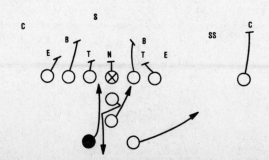

Figure 10-10 (continued)

60

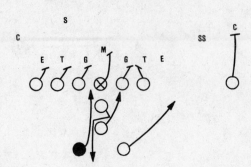

SPLIT FOUR

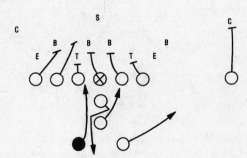

COLLEGE 4-3

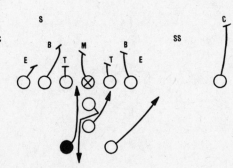

6-5 GOAL LINE

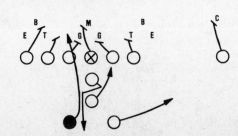

Quarterback Counter (Figure 10-11)
See Chapter 4 for rules and assignments.

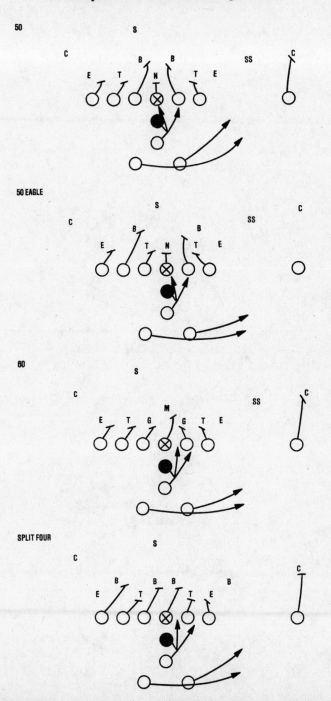

50

50 EAGLE

60

SPLIT FOUR

Figure 10-11 (continued)

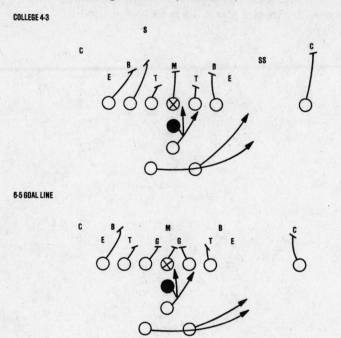

COLLEGE 4-3

6-5 GOAL LINE

Halfback Scissors (Figure 10-12)
See Chapter 4 for rules and assignments.

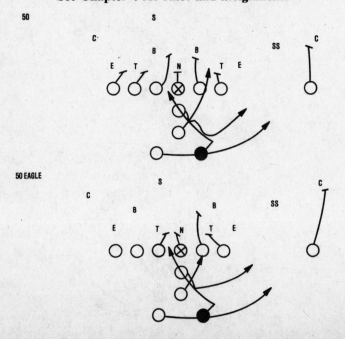

50

50 EAGLE

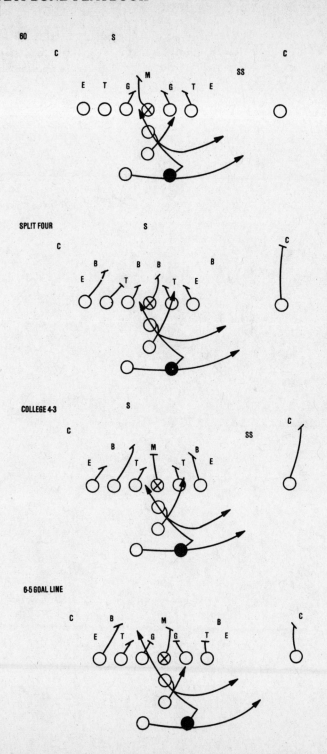

Common Counter-Blocking Adjustments (Figure 10-13)
Can be run with all inside counters (F.B.-Ctr., H.B.-Ctr., QB.-Ctr. and
H.B.-Scissors.) See Chapter 4 for rules, assignments and coaching points.

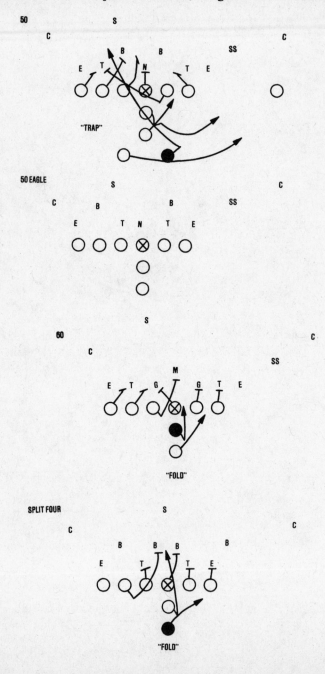

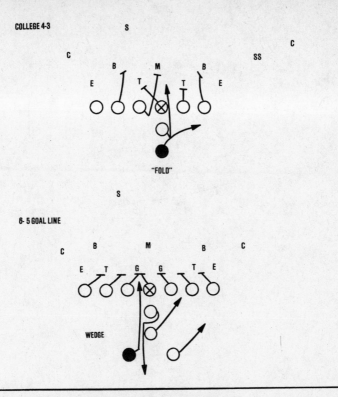

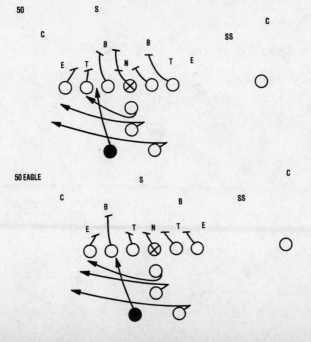

Counter Slant (Figure 10-14)
See Chapter 4 for rules, assignments and coaching points.

Figure 10-14 (continued)

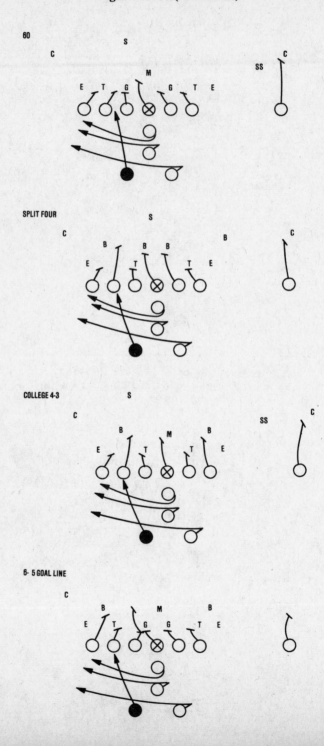

Counter Option (Figure 10-15)
See Chapter 4 for rules and assignments.

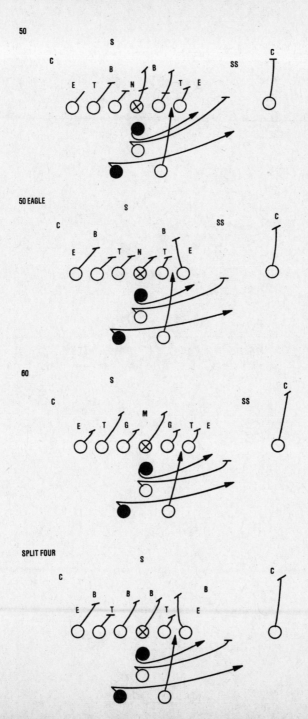

Figure 10-15 (continued)

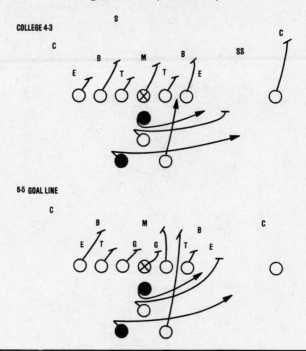

COLLEGE 4-3

6-5 GOAL LINE

Option Opposite (Figure 10-16)
See Chapter 4 for rules and assignments.

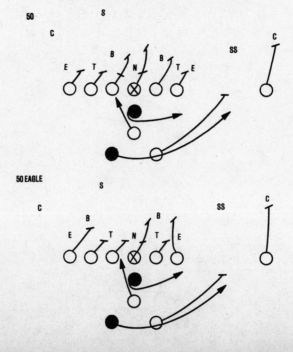

50

50 EAGLE

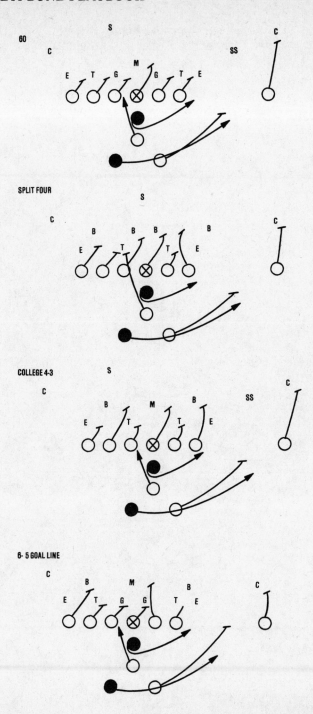

60

SPLIT FOUR

COLLEGE 4-3

6- 5 GOAL LINE

Sweep Opposite (Figure 10-17)
See Chapter 4 for rules and assignments.

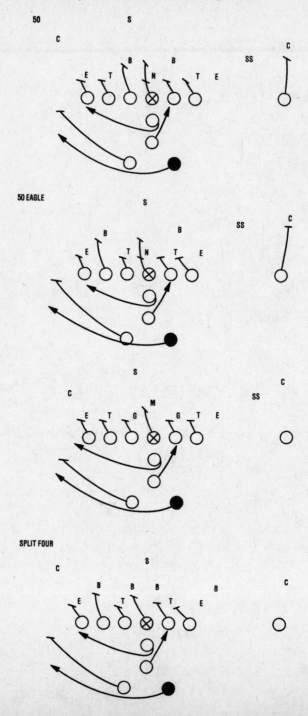

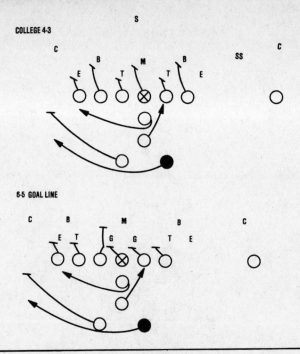

COLLEGE 4-3

6-5 GOAL LINE

Belly Opposite (Figure 10-18)
See Chapter 4 for rules and assignments.

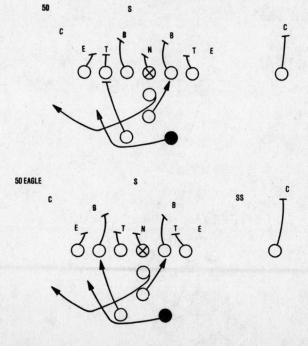

50

50 EAGLE

Figure 10-18 (continued)

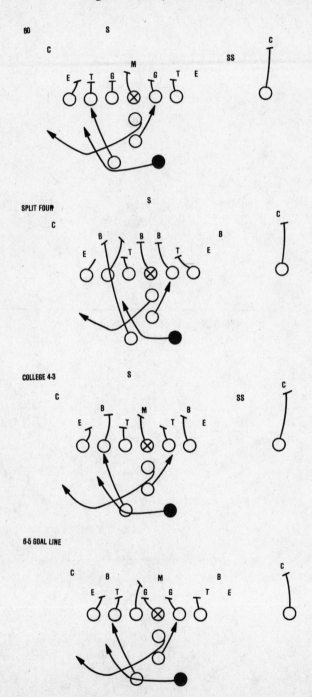

Fullback Counter—Halfbacks Opposite (Figure 10-19)
See Chapter 4 for rules and assignments.

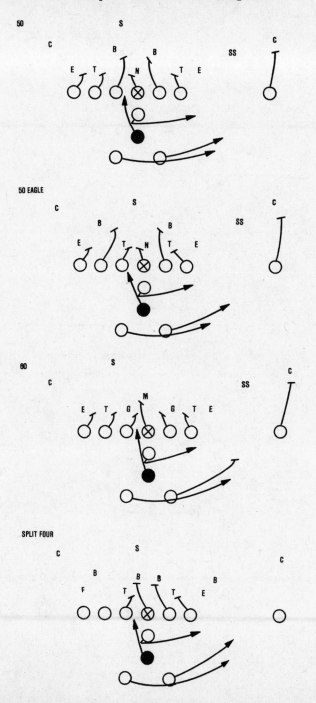

Figure 10-19 (continued)

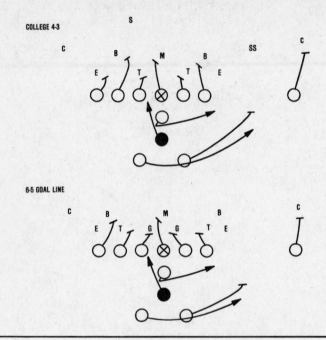

COLLEGE 4-3

6-5 GOAL LINE

Veer Opposite (Figure 10-20)
See Chapter 4 for rules, assignments and coaching points.

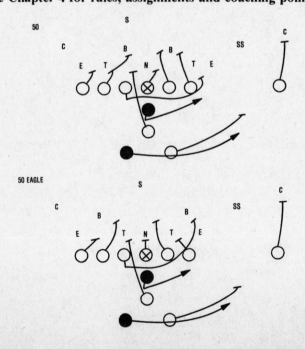

50

50 EAGLE

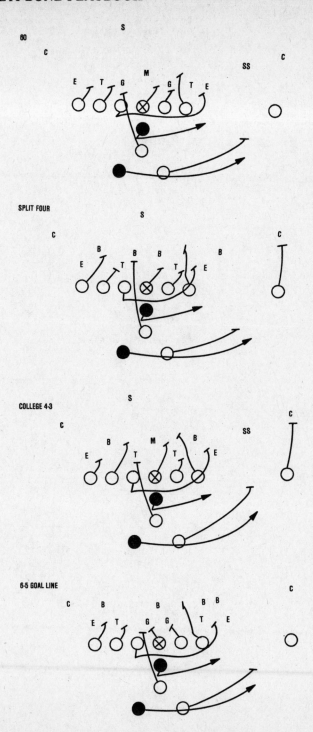

60

SPLIT FOUR

COLLEGE 4-3

6-5 GOAL LINE

Triple Pass (Figure 10-21)
See Chapter 6 for rules and assignments.

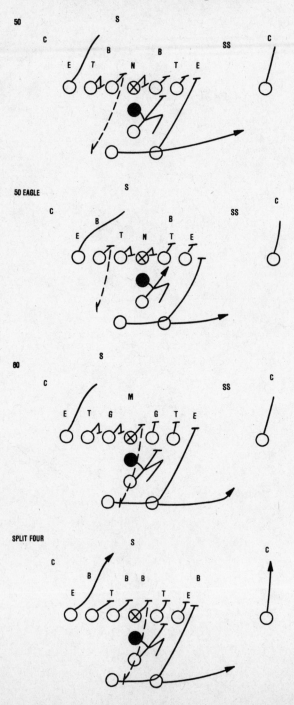

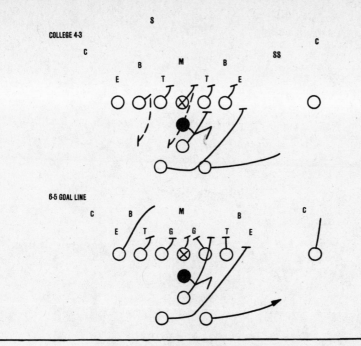

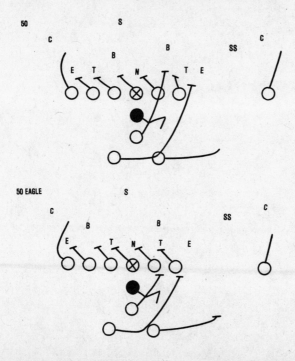

"Ice" Blocking (Figure 10-22)
See Chapter 6 for rules, assignments and coaching points.

Figure 10-22 (continued)

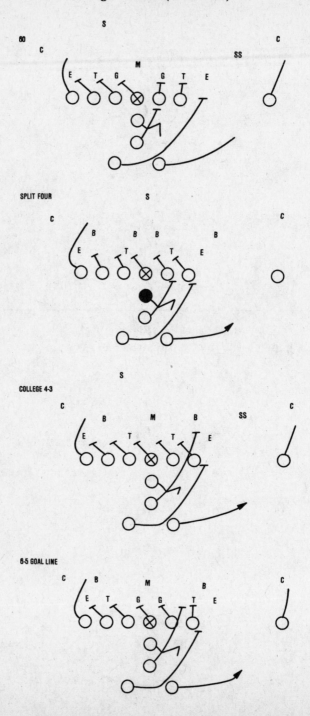

Belly Pass (Figure 10-23)
See Chapter 6 for rules and assignments.

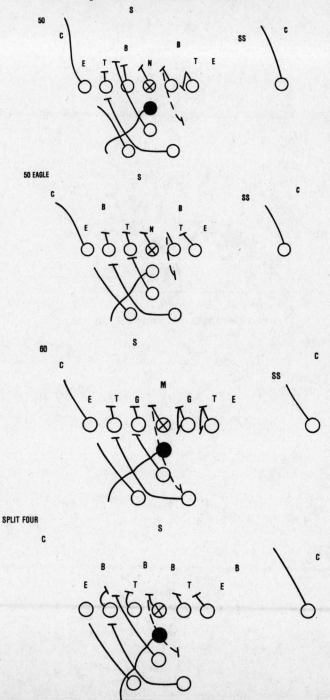

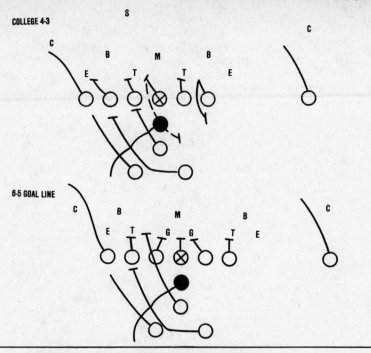

COLLEGE 4-3

6-5 GOAL LINE

Halfback Counter Pass (Figure 10-24)
Normal dropback blocking must be used!

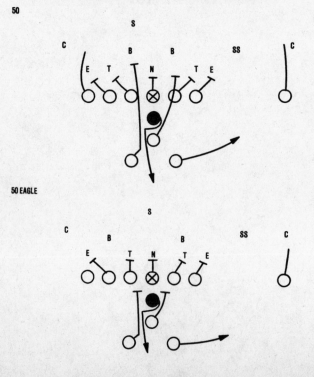

50

50 EAGLE

60

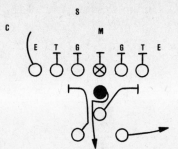

SPLIT FOUR

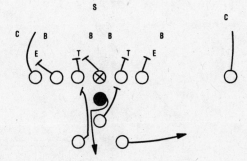

COLLEGE 4-3

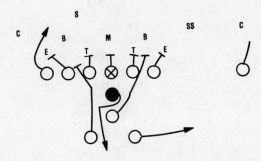

6-5 GOAL LINE

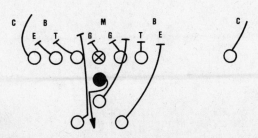

"MAX" MUST BE USED

Counter Option Pass (Figure 10-25)

50

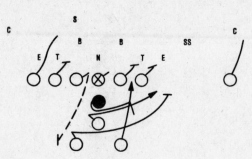

50 EAGLE

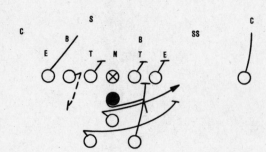

60

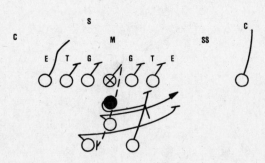

SPLIT FOUR

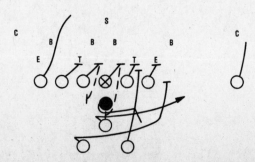

COLLEGE 4-3

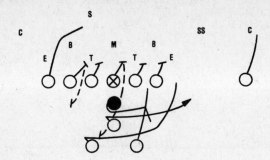

6-5 GOAL LINE

Option Dump Pass (Figure 10-26)
See Chapter 6 for rules, assignments and coaching points.

50 EAGLE

50

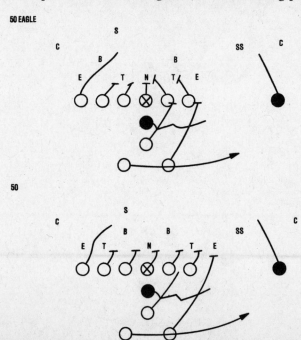

Figure 10-26 (continued)

60

SPLIT FOUR

COLLEGE 4-3

6-5 GOAL LINE

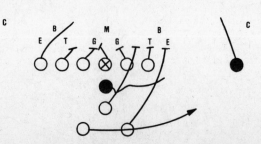

Option Opposite Dump Pass (Figure 10-27)
See Chapter 6 for rules, assignments and coaching points.

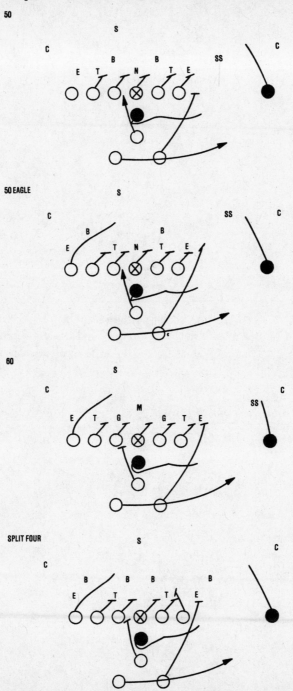

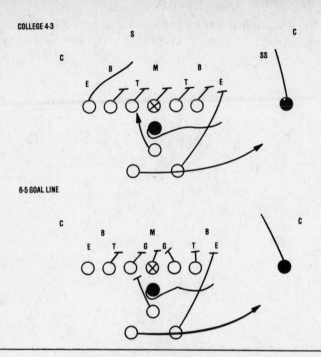

COLLEGE 4-3

6-5 GOAL LINE

Option Bootleg (Figure 10-28)
See Chapter 6 for rules, assignments and coaching points.

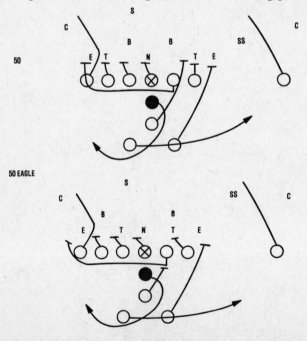

50

50 EAGLE

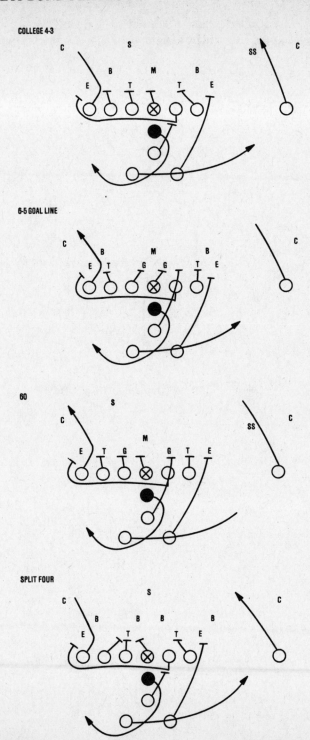

COLLEGE 4-3

6-5 GOAL LINE

60

SPLIT FOUR

Dropback Pass—"Normal" (Figure 10-29)
See Chapter 7 for rules, assignments and coaching points.

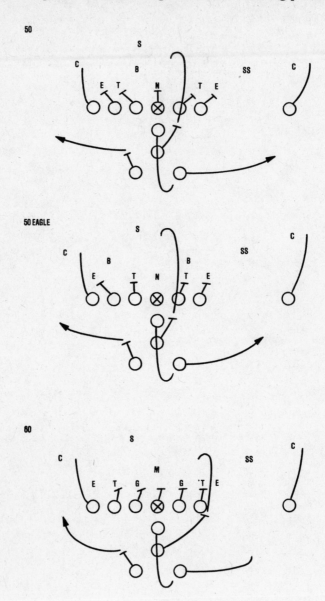

SPLIT FOUR

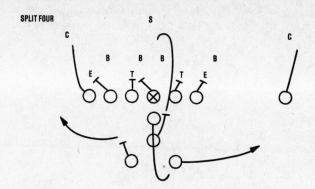

COLLEGE 4-3

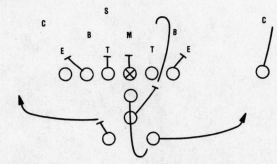

6-5 GOAL LINE

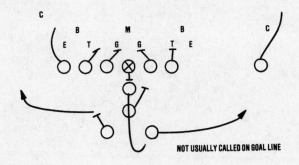

NOT USUALLY CALLED ON GOAL LINE

Dropback Pass—"Solid" (Figure 10-30)
See Chapter 7 for rules and assignments.

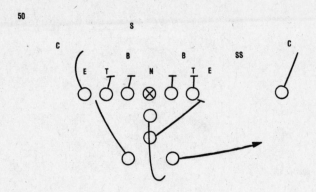

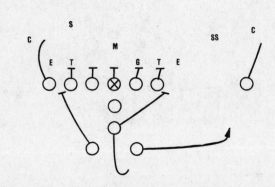

SPLIT FOUR

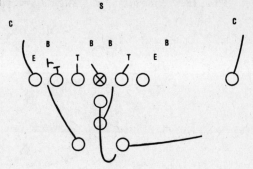

COLLEGE 4-3

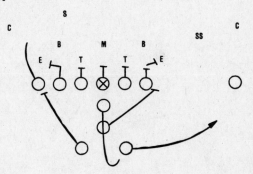

6-5 GOAL LINE

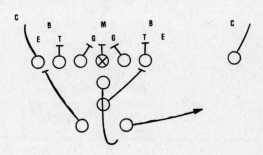

The Quick Draw (Figure 10-31)
See Chapter 7 for rules, assignments and coaching points.

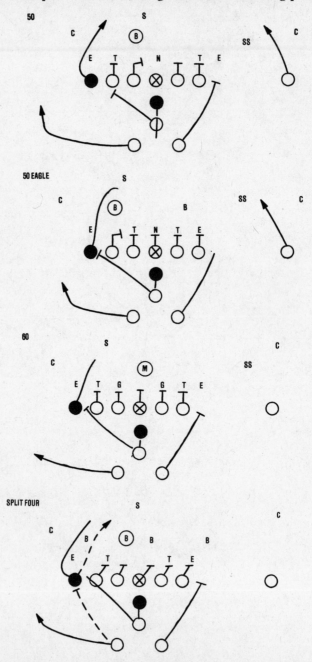

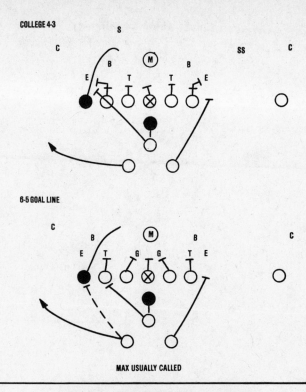

COLLEGE 4-3

6-5 GOAL LINE

MAX USUALLY CALLED

Sprint Out Pass (Figure 10-32)
See Chapter 8 for rules and assignments.

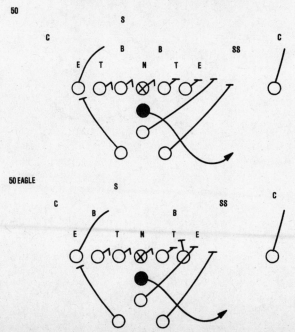

50

50 EAGLE

Figure 10-32 (continued)

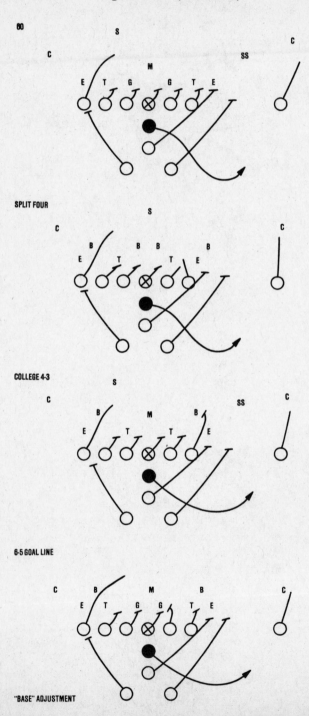

60

SPLIT FOUR

COLLEGE 4-3

6-5 GOAL LINE

"BASE" ADJUSTMENT

Sprint Draw (Figure 10-33)
See Chapter 8 for rules and assignments.

50

50 EAGLE

60

SPLIT FOUR

Figure 10-33 (continued)

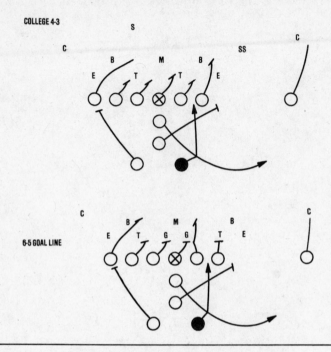

COLLEGE 4-3

6-5 GOAL LINE

Sprint Draw Pass (Figure 10-34)
See Chapter 8 for rules and assignments.

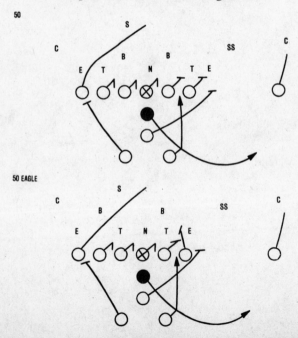

50

50 EAGLE

60

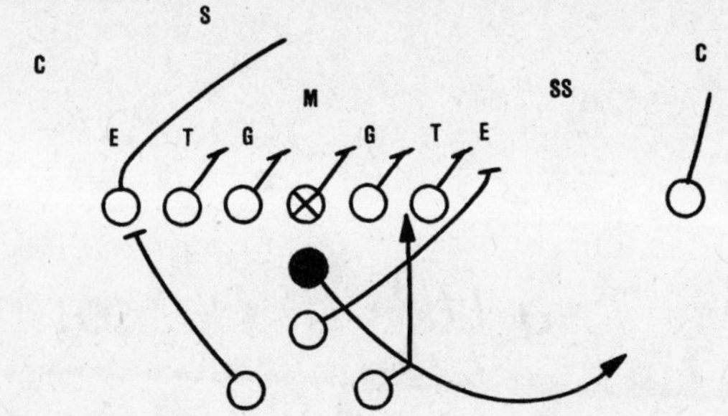

SPLIT FOUR

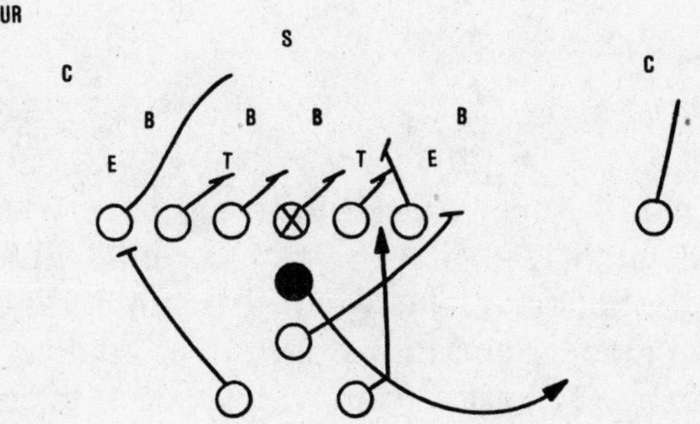

6-5 GOAL LINE

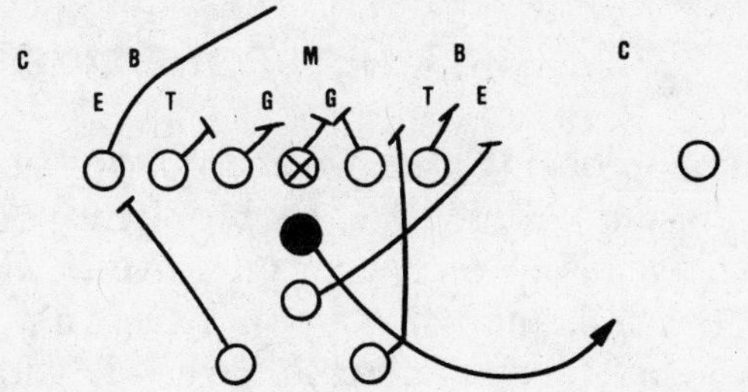

COLLEGE 4-3

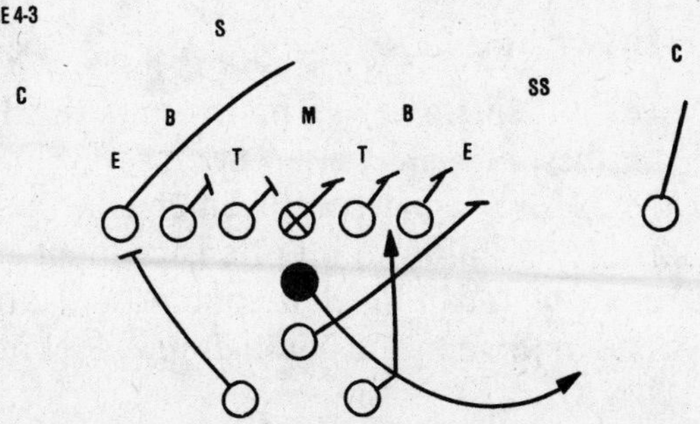

CHAPTER 11

The Use of Personnel
in the Multi-Bone

The Multi-Bone Attack, like every other offense, is dependent on the talent of the players on the squad. But the Multi-Bone provides the opportunity to win with flexibility and execution rather than talent alone. The Multi-Bone is the equalizer that will give any team a chance against a team with superior talent. When a Multi-Bone team has exceptional players, records are shattered and championships are won.

THE MULTI-BONE LINE

Multiple blocking schemes and quarterback execution of the triple option eliminate the need for big offensive linemen. Of course, it is advantageous to recruit an offensive tackle who is 6'5", 260, quick off the ball, and who can knock down houses. But a Multi-Bone team can still run an explosive attack with small linemen by relying on quarterback execution of his reads.

Placement on the Line

The five best linemen are not automatically placed at right guard, second best at tackle, etc. The *five best* linemen are inserted where needed. However, a super center is a must, and all things being equal, the best all-around offensive lineman is put at center. Having a center who can block a good nose guard one-on-one is a tremendous advantage in the Multi-Bone blocking schemes. Using the veer scheme, the onside guard can release directly on the offside backer rather than combo block on the nose guard. This enhances the potential of a "big play." The center is equally important in blocking the middle linebacker on an even front which again will increase the chances of breaking the long gain.

Requirements for the Offensive Line

The prime requirement for the Multi-Bone offensive lineman is the ability to get off the ball. If a line can explode off the ball, the offense will score. If they get off together, they will make things happen regardless of size. "Take-Off" must be practiced for a minimum of nine minutes daily. Quickness plus explosion will make great plays happen.

The next requirement is toughness. Toughness is the desire to stay with blocks until the whistle blows. As the title of this book suggests, this is an "explosive" attack, and for it to be explosive the linemen must go all out on every play. The difference between a ten-yard gain and a fifty-yard touchdown could be the downfield hustle of the "offside" line.

Strength in the legs and upper body is an absolute necessity for playing in the offensive line. It allows the linemen to knock people off the ball. An off-season "program" and in-season sled drills will help in this area.

If all the other requirements are present, size is the next consideration. It is no secret that a good, big man will beat a good, small man if everything else is equal.

THE RECEIVERS

For any attack to be explosive, its receivers must be able to catch the ball, run with it, and block. The passing game is an important part of the total offense. Without it there is no true multiplicity.

A minimum of four players are used as receivers; two split ends, the regular tight end who can also be a split end, and a second tight end who is a glorified tackle and is used in short yardage situations. Many coaches say, "We do not have all those players." NONSENSE! Receivers are waiting to be found in gym classes, on soccer fields, on basketball courts or on running tracks. Any player who has ever seen a football game would love to be a split end on our football team. Multi-Bone receivers do not have the heavy-duty blocking load that is common to most offenses. Therefore, the initial requirement to play as a receiver in the Multi-Bone attack is the ability to catch the football.

The next requirement is speed. The Multi-Bone must constantly present a deep threat to the opposing secondary, who should always fear being beaten deep. The faster the receiver, the greater vertical stretch and the greater the area to defend.

The requirements for tight end and split end differ.

Split Ends

The stalk block and crack block are extremely important to the success of the outside running attack, which is the heart of our explosiveness. The split ends must be able to make those blocks.

The ability to run with the football after he catches it can also add explosiveness to the attack. A run-talented third halfback could be used at wide receiver rather than on the bench.

Tight Ends

The biggest, strongest receiver goes to tight end. A talented blocker is needed at tight end to make blocks on the line of scrimmage (Belly block, TED, Hook, etc.) Although size is not a must requirement, blocking ability is. In addition, the tight end must stalk block and have the ability to catch the ball. The speed to go deep would be a plus and add to the explosiveness of the attack.

THE BACKFIELD

The importance of the running talents of the Multi-Bone backfield can never be underestimated. The best runners must be in the backfield.

The Fullback

The main requirement of the fullback position is quickness off the ball. The biggest mistake an option team can make is to put a big "bull" at fullback; one who can't get off the ball and single-handedly slows down the attack. Quickness at fullback beats the defensive tackle who tries to sit and read the hand-off.

The next requirement at the fullback spot is strength. Strength is not as important as quickness off the ball, but if a team has two quick fullbacks, then the stronger one should play.

Blocking ability at the fullback spot is very important, but Multi-Bone fullbacks do not have to make the difficult isolation block or the kick-out attack common to the I attack (Diagram 11-1). So there is no need for a glorified guard at fullback.

Due to the nature of our passing game the fullback must be able to catch the ball. Although he doesn't have to be a Lynn Swann, he should be a capable short receiver and be able to run strongly after the catch.

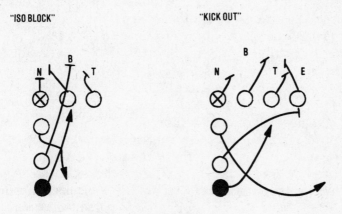

Diagram 11-1

The Halfbacks

The Multi-Bone halfbacks must be the most talented and gifted runners on the team. They must be game breakers. *Equally* important is outside speed. If the halfbacks are just talented but can't get outside, use them elsewhere. The fastest backs on the team are to be put at the halfback positions.

Blocking ability is especially important. The halfbacks' blocking is one of the success keys to the Multi-Bone running game. Blocking, however, can be taught—speed cannot. As long as a back has the desire to block, he can be taught how to block.

The final requirement for halfbacks is the ability to catch the football and, with their running talent, make yards after the catch.

Requirements for the Multi-Bone Quarterback

Regardless of what offense is used, the more talented the quarterback, the more successful the offense. The Multi-Bone, however, can be extremely effective regardless of the talent of the quarterback as long as he can contribute reading ability to the attack. The Multi-Bone quarterback has three ways of contributing to the success of the attack—by passing, by carrying the ball, or by reading of the options. A quarterback need not be a great passer or runner, but with hard work he can make a major contributions to the offense by mastering the reads. During the first season of the Multi-Bone, a defensive back was moved to quarterback. Though not a great passer (9 passes attempted per game) or runner (5 carries and 19 yards per game), he contributed to the offense by executing properly the triple option reads. The next year a new quarterback led the team in carries, in scoring, and passed 20 times per game. The Multi-Bone is easily adaptable to making the best use of your quarterback's strengths.

The most important asset for the Multi-Bone quarterback is his ability to read the defenses. This can be taught, but he must be willing to learn. If a quarterback cannot read defenses, he cannot play in the Multi-Bone offense. If he understands the offense and the defensive reaction against it, he can learn the necessary reads.

The passing game is an important part of the offense and its quarterback should have the ability to throw the ball. A quarterback who is not a great passer can be made effective by executing his passing reads. Though the converted defensive back threw only nine times per game, he threw completions for 620 yards because he understood and executed his reads.

Some coaches say, "We can't run the option because we do not have a running quarterback."—NONSENSE! Use the quarterback's strengths and stay away from his weaknesses. If the quarterback can pitch the ball and control the defensive end, he does not have to be a great runner. However, a running quarterback would be a big plus to the attack.

These then are the three talents desired at quarterback. A quarterback who is superior at all three would be awesome. The best pure passer always has the most potential and is worth working with in the other areas.

The only must-have physical requirement for the quarterback spot is agility.

ADJUSTING THE MULTI-BONE TO FIT PERSONNEL

Adjusting an attack philosophy to best use available talent is one of the main ingredients of coaching success. Maximizing strengths and overcoming weaknesses are easily accomplished by adapting the Multi-Bone Attack to fit the available personnel. This is made simple by the offense structure and its multiple format.

Adapting Blocking Schemes

The stronger the offensive line, the more base blocking is used. The power attack will be emphasized. Also, the use of wedge blocking and the fullback counter sequences will be stressed.

A small, quick line will need more help from the quarterback's reads of the triple option and variations of blocking schemes to produce better blocking angles and blocking success. Wedge and base blocking will not be used very often.

ADAPTING THE MULTI-BONE TO FIT
YOUR BACKFIELD STRENGTHS

The most important axiom for a successful Multi-Bone Attack is to give the ball to the best running back as many times as possible during a quarter, a game, a season.

Adjusting the Fullback

To stop a great fullback, defenses are required to pinch their tackles. Therefore, the fullback counter, with its various blocking schemes, becomes a big play. The opposite series will become very effective. the "dive read" from the triple option phase will be used more than usual to insure that the fullback gets the ball. Conversely, without a good fullback the "option read" will be called more often, and a few predetermined fullback plays will be called.

The one play that will become effective with a less talented player at fullback is the fullback counter with the halfbacks opposite, because the defense may overlook the fullback. The counter option with the fullback as a lead blocker should get additional use because the dive back is the halfback and the fullback is not required to be a running threat (Chapter 5). A mediocre fullback can contribute as a blocker and as a change-of-pace runner.

Regardless of his running ability, the defense must assign at least one man to take him on the triple option. This leaves one less defender to be blocked, and the fullback is contributing to the successful execution of the play without real running ability.

Adapting the Halfbacks

Facing two gifted halfbacks puts an unbelievable amount of pressure on a defense. They *must* get to carry the ball. Some Wishbone coaches complain that they can't get the ball to their halfbacks often enough. This is like an I formation coach saying he can't get the ball to his tailback. The following are some ways to give the Multi-Bone halfbacks the ball other than on the triple option:

1) The halfback counter.
2) The counter slant.
3) The sweep.
4) The belly.
5) The belly opposite.
6) The option opposite.
7) The sweep opposite.
8) The sprint draw.
9) The counter option.

These are nine ways to get the halfback the ball other than the basic triple option. Changing the blocking of each of these plays just once gives 18 ways to get the halfbacks the ball.

The triple option must be thought of as a pitch play, and with two gifted halfbacks a full bone would be used most of the time. Counter options and counter slants are good because the halfbacks are the running threats while the fullback is the lead blocker.

ONE GIFTED HALFBACK

With only one talented halfback, the Multi-Bone must insure that the defense doesn't take him away. There are many ways to give him the ball, and the bulk of the attack should be centered around him.

The main attack adjustment with only one good halfback available is to break the bone. The counter slant and the sprint draw become big plays especially from a heavy set. The Multi-Bone provides all the plays that would get an I tailback the ball, plus the counter slant. The sweep from a broken bone is a good way to get the halfback the ball (Diagram 11-2).

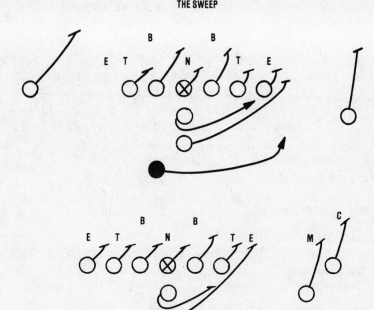

THE SWEEP

Diagram 11-2

WITHOUT A GIFTED HALFBACK

This is the worst possible situation to be in. The chance of being really explosive without halfbacks is absent because the pitch play will not be as effective. However, adjustments can be made.

The first adjustment is within the triple option. The "dive read" will be used more often. The quarterback should keep whenever possible and call for more load block schemes. The hook block will also help get the quarterback into the secondary.

Coaching Point: Don't totally abandon the pitch. Take it only when it is obvious and therefore has increased chance for success.

The halfbacks who are available can be used as threats by using the counter slant because it is a quick, north and south play and doesn't require great athletic ability. The counter attack phase will also become very fullback and quarterback-oriented (i.e., quarterback counters and fullback counters, etc.) when halfback talent is limited.

The passing game increases in importance. The dump passes become important and sprint pass action allows the use of the quarterback as a runner as well as a passer.

Without a superior halfback, the broken bone should be used to spread the defense. Heavy sets enhance the passing game by increasing the quarterback's threat on the sprint pass (see Chapter 8). Remember, to create explosiveness without gifted halfbacks, spread the defense and pass more often.

The Quarterback

The strengths of the quarterback will be the single most important factor in determining the character of your Multi-Bone. The more talented the quarterback, the greater the scoring potential. The Multi-Bone can adapt to fit any type of quarterback.

A GREAT RUNNING AND PASSING QUARTERBACK

The quarterback who can do it all will, of course, be highlighted by any offense. But caution should be used so that he is not overworked. Therefore, the triple option will be featured with all of the backs in the attack, and on the key downs load blocking will be used. All the backs should be established as running threats. Save the quarterback for the key times that spell game success. He should carry the ball about 12 to 20 times and throw about 20 passes per game.

ADAPTING TO THE QUARTERBACK'S RUNNING ABILITY

Breaking the bone is not suggested with a great running quarterback because it eliminates the load block. (Hook blocking can be used from a broken bone for the same effect.) With a running quarterback, the passing game will stress the dump passes, quick draw and the sprint pass. The predetermined run from the sprint pass action is a good call.

A quarterback with poor running ability should rarely call load blocking. Instead, he should pitch the ball as often as possible on all types of options.

The power attack becomes much more important if the quarterback has limited running ability, and the passing attack will feature the dropback game.

ADAPTING TO THE QUARTERBACK'S THROWING ABILITY

With a great passer, the following adjustments are obvious:

1) More passes are called.
2) Dropback action will be featured.
3) Use of more broken bone sets to get more receivers on the line of scrimmage for quick release into the secondary.

A poor throwing quarterback will cause the following adjustments:

1) Less total passes called.
2) More play action passes.
3) Sprint action rather than drop back.
4) Use of the full bone rather than broken bone sets

The Multi-Bone has the flexibility that allows you to adapt either year by year or week by week (injuries are still a part of football). It is an offense that any group of players can execute successfully regardless of their strengths or weaknesses.

CHAPTER **12**

Attacking Defenses with
the Multi-Bone

Preparation of game plans starts with analysis of the opponents' basic front. Its structure dictates the various ways they can defend the triple option.

The next step is to prepare for the various adjustments stemming from this front. The defensive front also dictates what secondary coverages to prepare for.

The particular personnel an opponent has at various positions will also have a strong bearing on the game plan. If the opponent has a defensive tackle who bears a strong resemblance to King Kong, run the other way.

GAME TIME ADJUSTMENTS

One of the great aspects of the Multi-Bone is that it has so many "built-in" cures for defensive adjustments. For example, an opponent's eight-man front can be reduced to a seven-man front by breaking the bone.

The first question to ask during the game is, "Are they stopping our triple option?" If they can't stop the triple option, they will get a very heavy dose of it. If they are defensing the triple option, then ask:

1) Who is tackling the fullback?
2) Who has the quarterback?
3) Who has the pitch?

4) Is the front being blocked?

5) Is the perimeter being blocked?

6) Are they getting extra people into the perimeter? If so, who?

7) What blocking adjustments should be made to run the triple?

After discovering how they are giving the triple option problems, attack the area that has been left weakened. For example, some teams will try to "fast-flow" their linebackers to get an extra defender in the perimeter (Diagram 12-1). This defensive tactic leaves the defense especially vulnerable to the counter attack.

The second question to be answered is, "How do they adjust to our multiple sets? Are they making sound adjustments?" At times a defense will make a recognition mistake or an error in adjusting to particular sets, which can create big-play situations.

Other areas that are charted are: How is our personnel matching up with the opponents? Can they be whipped on the line of scrimmage? Can the power attack be used? If the opponent's secondary is cheating to stop the run, then could the passing game produce a "quick six"?

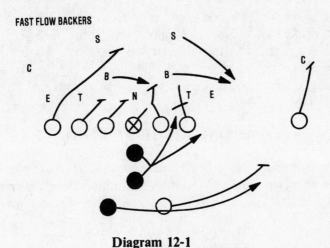

Diagram 12-1

Note: Never wait for the running game to be slowed down to begin to throw the ball. Take "home run" swings as often as there is sound reasoning for them. This is an *explosive* Multi-Bone attack. Never pass up a shot at a quick score.

Remember the main postulates for game adjustments are:

1) If there is a problem with the triple option, adjust the blocking.

2) If you are still having trouble with the triple (after altering the blocking), then run the triple from different sets.

3) If the triple still can't be established, attack the area where the defense is leaving itself vulnerable.

4) Always look for a shot at the quick touchdown.

5) Probe a defense to see how well they are prepared for multiple sets.

6) If a team is physically weak, use a greater selection of plays from the power attack.

7) If a defense is over-committed to the run, throw.

8) Always be conscious of using the passing game.

9) Always take advantage of defensive adjustments to the triple option.

CATEGORIZING DEFENSES

Defenses are classified as either seven- or eight-man fronts, then further broken down into odd and even fronts. The secondary is categorized first into three-man or four-man secondaries and then further classified by their run support (either invert or roll). Naturally, unbalanced defenses are put into a separate categories as are goal line defenses.

ATTACKING EIGHT-MAN FRONTS

Eight-man fronts have the obvious characteristic of eight men in the forcing unit and a three-man secondary. Whether it is an odd or even, the option responsibilities are basically the same:

1) Inside linebacker on the fullback.

2) Outside linebacker on the quarterback.

3) Defensive end on the pitch.

4) Corner has deep third. (Diagram 12-2)

There can be some change-ups. For example, the outside linebacker can play the pitch and the defensive end can take the quarterback. This has little effect because as long as the lead blocker stays on his path, he will block the defender responsible for the pitch.

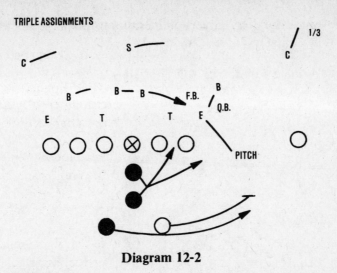

Diagram 12-2

Coaching Point: A split-six defense does not have as much flexibility because it does not have an outside linebacker.

Another very unsound scheme that can be taken advantage of is (Diagram 12-3):

1) Outside linebacker on the fullback.
2) Defensive end on the quarterback.
3) Corner on the pitch.
4) Safety to the deep outside.

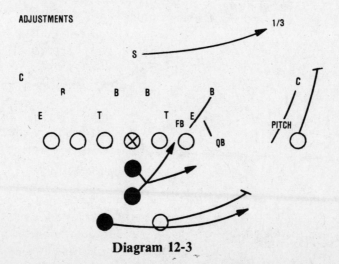

Diagram 12-3

This leaves the defense very vulnerable to a simple streak pass to the split end (Diagram 12-4).

Coaching Point: The split end should take a 17-yard split against an eight-man front.

THE STREAK VS ROTATION

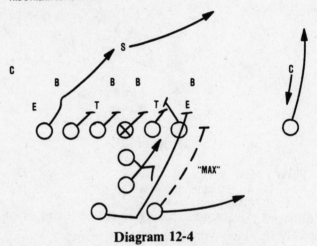

Diagram 12-4

Another possible defensive adjustment is inverting the safety to the pitch (Diagram 12-5). This leaves the secondary in poor position to defend the post to the split end or the throwback post to the tight end (Diagram 12-6). This can produce a quick TD.

THE POST VS INVERT

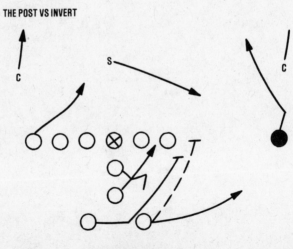

Diagram 12-5

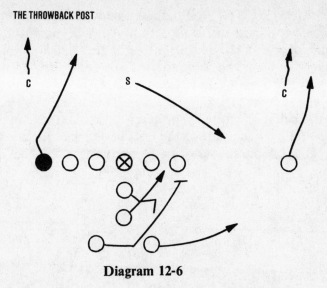

Diagram 12-6

The 5.3 defense is an odd eight-man front. This has the characteristics of the other eight-man fronts, but there is a man on the center. This makes it very difficult to tackle the fullback from the inside (Diagram 12-7).

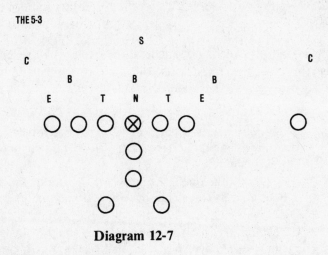

Diagram 12-7

Defeating the Split Four

The most popular eight-man front is the Split Four. The principles for attacking eight-man fronts are always the same;

ESTABLISH THE TRIPLE OPTION. The Split Four is not equipped to handle the triple option. An eight-man front cannot get enough people in the perimeter to stop the triple option. If the lead blocker can block the man responsible for the pitch, lots of yardage will be gained until they make a change.

The quarterback does not have to read a Split-Four. He can give the ball to the fullback on every play since the man responsible for the fullback is inside of the offensive tackle. He can always pull the ball and pitch *unless* both the outside linebacker and the defensive end play pitch (Diagram 12-8).

TWO ON PITCH

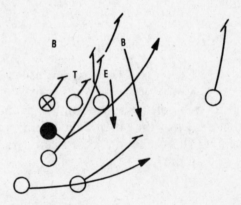

Diagram 12-8

If the lead blocker is not successfully executing the lead block, then use the Twin Bone. (Also use the Twin Bone just as a change of pace.) Adjustments that the defense might make are:

1) Moving the outside linebacker out on the slot. This eliminates a cross charge between the defensive end and the outside backer (Diagram 12-9). This is a common adjustment.

2) Sliding all the linebackers toward the slot making the Split Four a Four-Three and thus a seven-man front (Diagram 12-10).

3) Cheating the safety on the slot. This could really leave them vulnerable to deep passes or weakside runs. (Diagram 12-11).

Coaching Points:
1) The blocking patterns will vary and include "X" blocking, load blocks, and TED blocks;

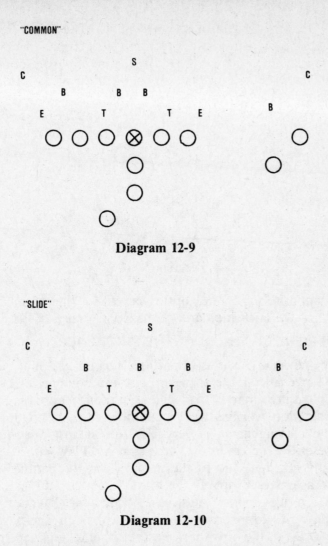

Diagram 12-9

Diagram 12-10

2) The fullback can be used as a battering ram against the split four and should carry at least a dozen times to keep the defense honest.

THE COUNTER ATTACK VS. THE SPLIT FOUR

Because the inside linebacker in a Split Four is assigned to take the fullback, he must react to flow as quickly as possible. This opens up the inside counter game completely. All the inside counters, with various blocking schemes, will be effective (see Chapter 4).

The Split Four needs secondary help to stop the pitch. The

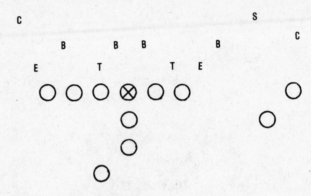

Diagram 12-11

option opposite and counter option can exploit their secondary flow and attack the backside flank of the Split Four (see Playbook).

THE POWER ATTACK VS. THE SPLIT FOUR

The power attack is used sparingly against the Split Four due to the effectiveness of the triple option and counter attack. Some power plays are run to keep the offense as multiple as possible. If the power attack is working well, it can be used more often.

The passing game is very effective against the Split Four because of the success of the running game. Play action passes are especially effective due to the weakness in the perimeter of the defense against the run. If the playside corner starts to become involved in run support, the streak is wide open (Diagram 12-4). If the safety tries to invert to help against the run, the post can be effective, as can the throwback post to either the tight end or to the split end (Diagram 12-5). These are the types of passes that produce quick touchdowns. From the Twin Bone, the dump pass to the slot could also produce a big gain (Diagram 12-12).

The dropback pass can be devastating if they try to adjust to the Twin Bone with their safety.

Coaching Points:
1) Against a Split Four, spread the secondary and throw away from the safety.
2) The streak is especially tough to defend (Diagram 12-13).

SLOT DUMP

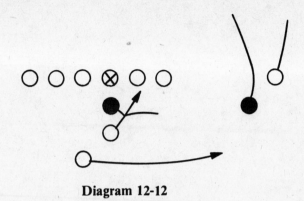

Diagram 12-12

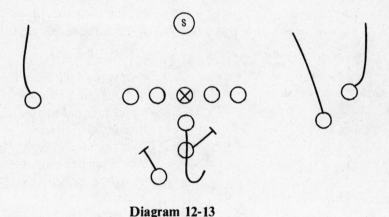

Diagram 12-13

The sprint pass can also be troublesome to a Split Four especially if the quarterback breaks containment "Sprint 70" is a good possession play run from the Heavy Twin Bone (Diagram 12-14). The quarterback reads the outside linebacker:

1)   If he takes the flat, the quarterback throws to the curl.
2)   If the outside backer drops to curl, he hits the out.
3)   If both are covered, the quarterback runs.

"SPRINT 70"

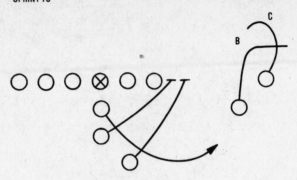

Diagram 12-14

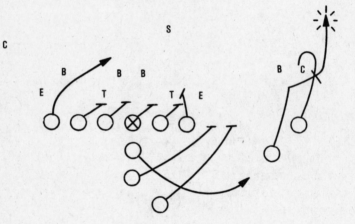

Diagram 12-15

Note: If the corner is coming up to play flat, throw the out and up (Diagram 12-15).

The throwback flare isolates the backside linebacker on the halfback and tight end on the corner (Diagram 12-16).

Coaching Point: The quarterback throws to the halfback unless the outside linebacker covers him. If the outside backer takes the halfback, the tight end is open: a) the inside linebackers should react to flow; b) the backside corner must play the deep third.

THROWBACK FLARE"

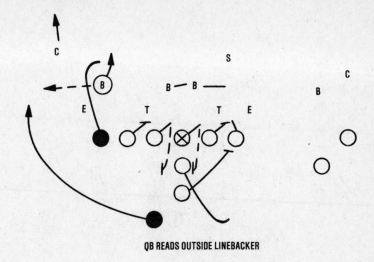

QB READS OUTSIDE LINEBACKER

Diagram 12-16

Though the running game is effective, plan to throw the ball 20 times or more against an eight-man front. The combination of the pass and an option attack puts too much pressure on the eight-man front's perimeter to allow really successful defense.

ATTACKING SEVEN-MAN FRONTS

The Oklahoma (50) and the Sixty are the most common seven-man fronts. The only difference between a 50 and a 60 is the position of the defenders over the guards and center (Diagram 12-17). Their alignment does not change the total approach to the game plan except for the following adjustments against a 60:

1) More veer blocking to get a combo block on the defender on our guard.
2) Use of the "opposite attack" to get a better block on the middle linebacker.
3) The fold blocking scheme will be used on the counter phase of the attack.

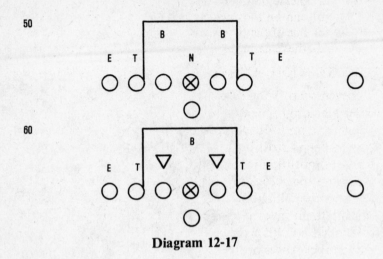

DIFFERENCE BETWEEN 50 & 60

Diagram 12-17

Characteristics of Seven-Man Fronts

The basic characteristics of seven-man fronts are (Diagram 12-18)

1) Seven men in the forcing unit.

2) Four-man secondary that can either rotate or invert into a three- or two-deep secondary.

3) The fullback will usually be taken by a defender outside the tackle's block.

OPTION RESPONSIBILITIES—50 & 60

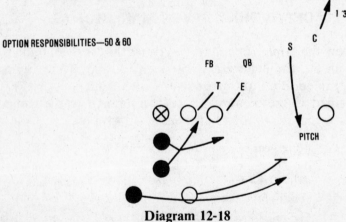

Diagram 12-18

4)   The triple option will be defended:
   a) tackle on the fullback;
   b) end on the quarterback;
   c) one of the two secondary people to play on the side pitch
   d) the remaining secondary man is assigned to the deep third.

TRIPLE OPTION AGAINST A SEVEN-MAN FRONT

A seven-man front *cannot* hold up to the triple option with multiple blocking schemes. The triple option pins down four defenders (one on fullback, one on quarterback, one on pitch, and one on the deep third) but still has a lead blocker who blocks the defender responsible for the pitch.

Varying the blocking on the perimeter causes additional problems to the Oklahoma defense. The crack block is absolutely devastating to an inverting safety. He is faced with the dilemma of being blocked by either the lead blocker or the wide receiver. The load block also causes problems for a defensive end who is assigned the quarterback, and it destroys the "invert-on-quarterback" stunt. If teams continue to use the invert-on-quarterback stunt, the hook block can be very effective.

Changing the sets can alter blocking patterns and present another problem to the perimeter defense. For example, by using a Pro Bone, the tight end has the responsibility of blocking the defender responsible for the pitch. But by switching to the Twin Bone, the man responsible for the pitch must come out on the slot, which eliminates the invert-on-quarterback stunt.

ATTACKING THE OKLAHOMA ADJUSTMENTS

When the triple option is being run successfully against the Oklahoma 50, the defense must get one more defender into the perimeter in addition to the original four. Which defender they are trying to put in the perimeter will determine how our attack will adjust.

The Invert on Quarterback Stunt

The invert-on-quarterback stunt puts the safety on the quarterback, while the defensive end fires upfield for the pitch (Diagram 12-19). The thinking behind this stunt is that the

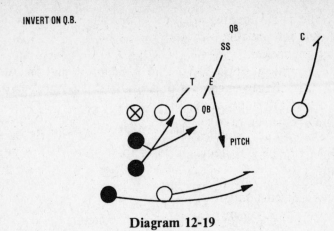

INVERT ON Q.B.

Diagram 12-19

quarterback will read and keep (because of the end firing upfield), turn upfield, and the safety will make the tackle.

The normal triple option defeats this stunt as long as the lead blocker stays on his path. The quarterback can see this stunt coming before the snap and should be prepared for it.

The dump pass to the split end side also discourages this stunt. Other ways of beating this stunt are:

1) load blocking;
2) hook blocking;
3) using the Twin Bone.

The major point here is that the triple option with the lead blocker can handle this stunt, but the multiplicity of the attack can give other ways to take advantage of it.

The Scrape Stunt

The scrape stunt is an attempt to put an extra defender in the perimeter. This maneuver puts the defensive tackle down on the fullback while the linebacker scrapes to the quarterback or the pitch (Diagram 12-20).

Again, the triple option has a built-in adjustment to this stunt. With veer blocking, the tackle blocks the defensive tackle down while the fullback, just by following his veer blocking rules, will get outside and pick off the scraping backer.

Zone or X blocking are perfect calls against this stunt, and the belly play can produce sizable gains because the lead blocker picks off the linebacker.

The option opposite with multiple blocking schemes also proves very effective against this stunt because the misdirection will slow down the linebacker's flow. All the counters, with multiple blocking schemes, take advantage of quick-flowing backers.

The Shooting Nose Guard

Firing the nose guard to either guard-center gap is another tactic the defense might use to get another player to the side of the triple option (Diagram 12-21).

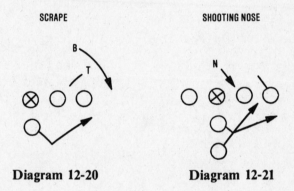

SCRAPE	SHOOTING NOSE

| Diagram 12-20 | Diagram 12-21 |

Veer blocking successfully handles this stunt because of the double team on the nose guard. The fullback and quarterback counters should produce big plays against this stunt.

Safety Cheating to a Side

If a defense is given major problems by the triple option, it may get radical and try to cheat the safety to the wide side; the corner and the strong safety will both fire upfield (Diagram 12-22).

The best method of combating this stunt is the "check with me" call and attacking away from the safety. If the triple is run toward the safety, the split end will block the corner, the lead back the monster, and the pitch back will have half the field to beat the safety (Diagram 12-23).

The passing game will also provide problems for a cheating safety (see the Playbook, Chapter 10).

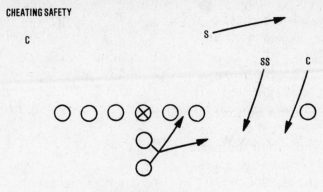

CHEATING SAFETY

Diagram 12-22

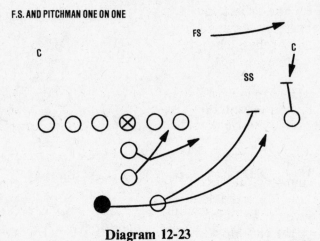

F.S. AND PITCHMAN ONE ON ONE

Diagram 12-23

The Oklahoma defense can be devastated by the Multi-Bone as long as constant attention is paid to how it is attempting to get the extra defender into the perimeter. This defensive adjustment will automatically determine which phase of the Multi-Bone to use (see Analysis Sheet at the end of this chapter.)

ATTACKING THE GOAL LINE

The most common goal line defense is the 65. Holding the fullback to less than three yards per attempt is an almost impossible task for this defense.

The tight formation is a Multi-Bone standard when in a goal

line situation because of the additional blocking strength. The only time a broken bone set is used is if the lead blocker is having problems.

The Triple Option on the Goal Line

The triple option with the "dive read" is the most difficult play in football to stop for less than three yards. Veer blocking successfully seals the inside crease for the fullback, and the fullback is instructed to "be your own blocker." The quarterback, knowing the situation, will give to the fullback the majority of the time unless he is sure the defensive tackle can make the play.

The outside dimension of the play is just as difficult to defend because the cornerback must respect the tight end as a receiver. The lead blocker, by staying on his path, will pick off the defender responsible for the pitch and the running back heads for the goal line getting positive yardage.

> **Coaching Point:** Even a poor job of blocking the perimeter will produce three yards because there are three offensive people to only two defensive people (see the Playbook, Chapter 10).

Blocking Adjustments

The most useful blocking adjustment for the triple option in a goal line situation is the "load" call. This adjustment makes the triple either a give to the fullback or a quarterback keep.

The tight end blocking adjustments on the goal line are also effective. The TED block can seal the outside linebacker and allow the lead blocker to block the corner (who may be easier to handle). The hook block is used to free the lead blocker on the corner and eliminate the possibility of firing the defensive and upfield.

The triple option, with only these three adjustments, provides a goal line offense in itself.

THE BELLY PLAY VS. THE GOAL LINE

The defensive tackle cannot stop the fullback for less than three yards and successfully defend the belly play. Because he must fire down on the fullback, base blocking will be very effective. The only adjustment made with the belly is to TED block. TED blocking changes the assignments of the tight end and lead blocker, which may make an easier block for the lead blocker.

THE OPTION OPPOSITE

The middle linebacker flowing with the fullback causes the success of the option opposite. The same blocking adjustments used for the triple option are used for the option opposite (load, TED, and hook).

THE HALFBACK COUNTER

If the middle backer flows with the fullback, he cannot make the play on the halfback counter. The only adjustment for this play is wedge blocking (the halfback is told to leap over the line of scrimmage). The quarterback tries to get the ball to the halfback as deep as possible to allow him to take off quickly.

QUARTERBACK OR FULLBACK WEDGE

If the ball is inside the one yard line the fullback counter with wedge blocking is tough to stop, as is the quarterback counter with wedge blocking which is, in essence, a quarterback sneak.

Passing on the Goal Line

The passing game is not often used in a goal line situation because the great success of the running game usually makes it unnecessary.

THE DUMP PASS

The most used play action pass on the goal line is the dump pass. The outside linebacker will probably take the pitch and leave the "quickie" to the tight end open. If not, the load block will allow the quarterback to run for the required minimum three yards. Throwing the dump to the end is also effective.

THE SPRINT PASS

In obvious passing downs, the sprint pass is very difficult to defend. If the situation is an obvious passing one, a heavy broken bone set may be used. Two most often used routes are the slant and "V" out to the split end. The quarterback is instructed to run if at all in doubt. The sprint pass is effective on the goal line because:

1) The quarterback is a threat to run for the score.
2) The corner can't play both the quarterback and the out route.
3) Releasing a back into the pattern (either on a flare or an out) causes an additional problem for the outside linebacker. (Diagram 12-24)

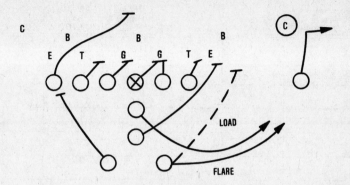

SPRING RIGHT "O"

Diagram 12-24

The full bone with two tight ends is the most powerful goal line attack known. Some teams use the Wishbone only in goal line situations, The Multi-Bone affords the luxury of using the "tight set" on the goal line while using the rest of the offense in other situations.

ANALYSIS SHEET

PLAY #	DOWN DISTANCE	YD. LINE	FORMATION	PLAY	GAIN	BALL CARRIER # POSITION	TACKLE BY # POSITION	COMMENT

GAME PLAN _____ ON _____ DATE _____

NORMAL DOWNS			OBVIOUS LONG		OBVIOUS SHORT		GOAL LINE		
1st & 10	2nd & 5-7	3rd & 2-3	1 & 10 + 2 & 7 +	3rd & 4 +	1 & –10 2 & –5	3rd & –2			
							1st & 4 +	1st & 2 +	1st & –2
							2nd & 2-4 +	2nd & 2-4	2nd & –2
							3rd & 4 +	3rd & 2-4	3rd & –2
							4th & 4 +	4 & 2-4	4 & –2
							GOAL LINE SPECIALS		

INDEX